DRUG SMUGGLING AND TAKING IN INDIA AND BURMA

First published 1922
This edition published by Lector House in 2024

ISBN: 978-93-6138-499-8

Lector House LLP
Registered Office: H. No. 96, Block C, Tomar Colony,
Burari, Delhi – 110084, India
info@lectorhouse.com
www.lectorhouse.com

DRUG SMUGGLING AND TAKING IN INDIA AND BURMA

ROY K. ANDERSON

2024

LECTOR HOUSE LLP

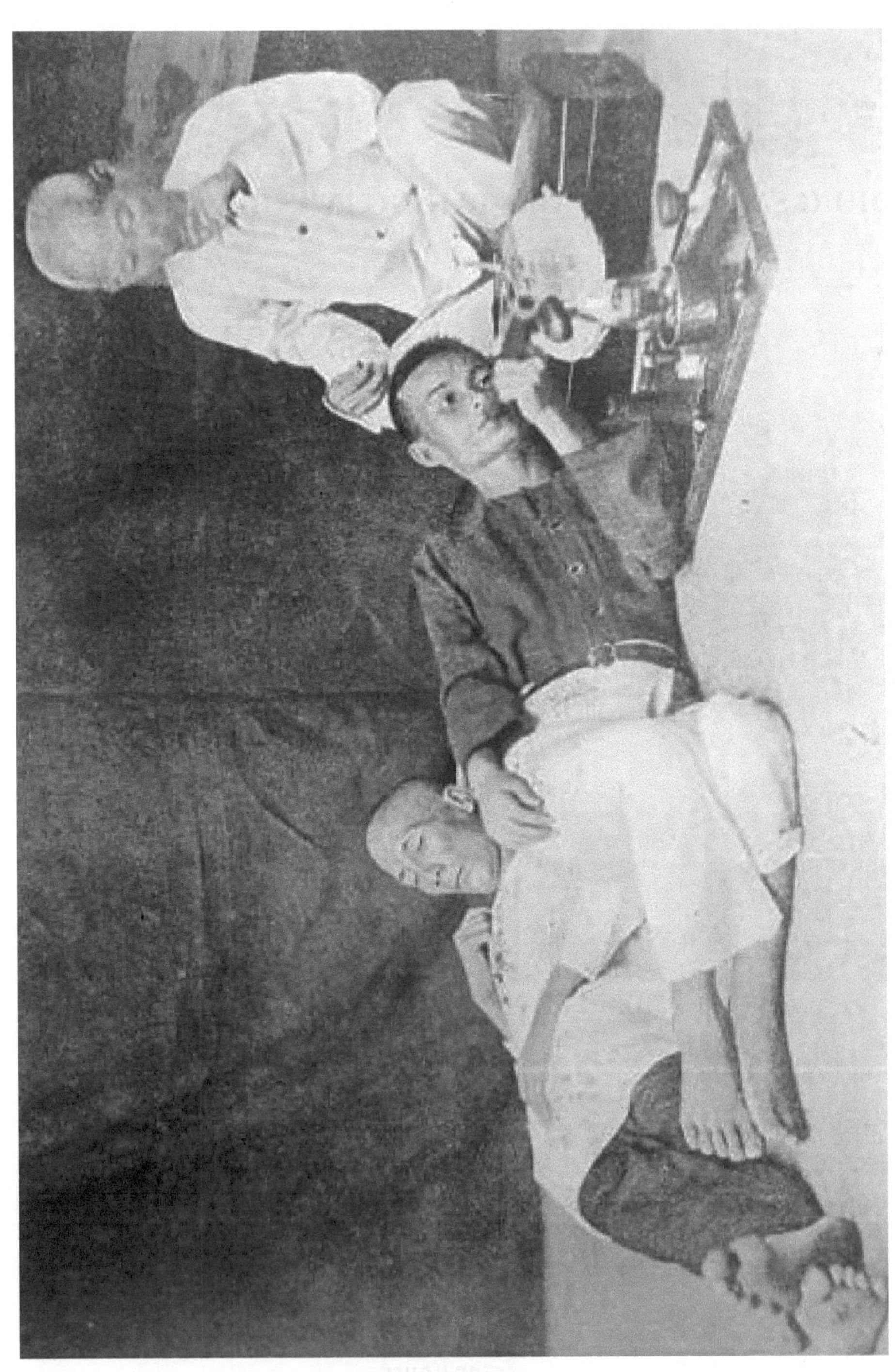

Group of Opium Smokers

DRUG SMUGGLING AND TAKING IN INDIA AND BURMA

BY

ROY. K. ANDERSON, F.R.S.A.

Superintendent, Burma Excise Department

*"So deep the power of these ingredients pierced
Even to the inmost seat of mental sight"*—PARADISE LOST

ILLUSTRATED

Preface.

At a time when the drug-evil, as it is called, is attracting so much attention all over the world, it does not seem out of place to tell the public something about how conditions in regard to it obtain in India and Burma. As far as I have been able to ascertain there is no literature on this subject outside "blue books," and those admirable compilations are notoriously dry reading. A novel called "*Dope*" by Sax Rohmer professes to deal with the drug-evil and the traffic in drugs in the West; but it is a novel; has a hero, a heroine, a forbidding type of detective, and some degenerates, and a few impossible Chinamen in it, to give verisimilitude to the title and all that it implies.

I do not profess to write as an authority on the subjects I have taken up. I realise that there are scores of others more experienced, and infinitely better able to make a book on these subjects than I am; but there seems to be little hope of their ever getting the better of their modesty and appearing in print. I write of what I have seen for myself, and ventilate opinions I have formed which I expect no one to subscribe to who differs from them. My readers may rest assured, however, that what I relate is true. I have not consciously exaggerated, nor have I suppressed facts. I write on a subject in which I am interested; and, if the attention that has at different times been given to my verbal accounts is an indication of something more than the polite toleration of the raconteur, then there are others also who are interested, and I need offer no apologies for my attempt to supply a deficiency in the bookshelves of those who want more information.

A preface often affords the writer an opportunity of performing a pleasant duty. That which I have to perform is to record my thanks to Mr. F. W. Dillon, Barrister, and author of "*From an Indian Bar Room*," for the trouble he took in reading the manuscript, and his many helpful suggestions.

R. K. ANDERSON.

REDFERN,
26*th March,* 1921.

Contents

APPENDIX.

List of Illustrations

SMUGGLING.

Chapter I.

Smuggling and Smugglers.

Everybody is a smuggler at heart!

Our innate free-trade instincts and love of liberty revolt against what we look upon as uncalled for interference with our rights when we are called upon to declare and pay duty on a box of cigars or a bottle of whisky when we disembark at a Customs port; and we look upon evasions of these obligations, not as evidences of moral obliquity, but as a very proper exercise of the exemption which we claim as our right. On the whole, this point of view is to be sympathized with, and in the case of such innocuous articles as laces, scent, and feathers, it is to be excused; the mysteries of the revenue law, and the underlying principles of taxation, are unfamiliar to most of us. But a greater degree of culpability must be attached to those who seek to evade the law by the illicit importation of articles whose unrestricted use produces nothing but harm; and while the former class of delicts may be classed as mere revenue offences, the latter must be treated as crimes and severely punished as such.

It is in the nature of things that articles which have come to be looked upon as necessaries of life, such as tea, tobacco, wine and spirits, should be taxed moderately; and indeed, were any attempt made to render them less easily obtained by raising the taxes on them, unless this course was vital in the interests of the country, there would be just reasons for profound popular dissatisfaction and disgust; but in the matter of noxious intoxicating drugs the case is reversed, and authoritative opinion inclines to the highest taxation, or even to total prohibition. Opium is taxed to a point little short of prohibition; morphia and cocaine are entirely prohibited to the public except for medical purposes; and hemp drugs are highly taxed in India, and totally prohibited in Burma. Those who quarrel with this state of things are such as have become habituated to these drugs, and of this class there is, unhappily, a large number, so large a number indeed, that their demand for a regular and sufficient supply constitutes a rich market, a market which is supplied by the smuggler who reaps abundant profits.

As in the case of other articles of commerce—and smuggling is as much a branch of commerce as the traffic in rice or jute—the scarcity or abundance of supply of drugs is what regulates their price in the illicit market. Normally, opium is sold from Government Opium Shops at from Rs. 100 to Rs. 123 a seer. Illicitly, it costs from Rs. 200 to Rs. 300 a seer, and when scarce, from Rs. 350 to Rs. 400 a seer. Illicitly, cocaine and morphia are sold at from five to six times the chemist's price. It is true that the smuggler has to pay and maintain a large staff of assistants, and has to bear other heavy expenses, but the net profit he eventually gets is a very substantial one.

It is impossible to entirely prevent smuggling: the interested motives of mankind will always prompt them to attempt it. All that the Government can do is to compromise with an offence which, whatever the criminal law on the subject may say, appears to the mind of the smuggler, and of the drug habitué he supplies, as not at all equalling in turpitude those acts which are clear breaches of the elementary principles of ethics.

To the generality of people the smuggler is a bold, bad man with a fierce, heavily-whiskered face, and armed to the teeth with knives, pistols, and other lethal accoutrements. His surroundings are a rugged cliff, with a roaring surf at its feet; while a dimly lit cave, stocked with barrels of spirit and bales of tobacco, completes the mental picture. In reality the smuggler—the Indian smuggler at any rate—is nothing of the sort. To all appearances he is a respectable, well-to-do, easy-going merchant with a flourishing business in piece-goods, rice, or timber. But he is a thorough-paced smuggler for all that, and his business is merely a blind to his real occupation which is the importation and traffic in opium, cocaine, morphia, and hemp-drugs. It is this business which is the real source of his wealth; it is his mind that directs and accomplishes great ventures in smuggling.

To be successful as a smuggler, a man needs to have more than ordinary ability. His powers of organization, and the ability to rapidly appreciate a situation, must be of the first order, and in addition, he must be endowed with an unusually large measure of low cunning and deceit. It is true that the smuggler's plans sometimes miscarry, but this is usually owing to treachery on the part of one of his assistants. The possibility of such treachery exemplifies the need the smuggler has for a strong personality and ability to judge character, and appraise men at their true worth; its infrequency testifies to the possession by smugglers of these qualities in an unusual degree.

It must not be supposed that the smuggler takes a very active part in his nefarious traffic; it is doubtful whether he ever sees the drugs for the importation of which he is responsible. His assistants look to all minor details, he only supplying the necessary money, and directing operations as a general directs an army in the field. His host of underlings realise only too well how relentless would be the fate that would overtake them were they to "give away" their employer, for those who have proved faithless to their trust have not survived long enough to enjoy the fruits of their perfidy! The faithful ones know they have nothing to lose or fear. Fines are paid by their employer, and jail has no terrors for them, because their families are provided for by the smuggler while they are away, and they return to their employment and the society of their companions after release from a course of hard, healthful, muscle-forming labour.

So far I have dealt exclusively with the man who smuggles in a large and extended way. He might be likened to the big importer of ordinary business. But, as in ordinary business, there are the retailers: those who take the goods to the consumer. These men operate up-country, in the sense that they work in the interior of the country. They may be agents of the big men, or they may be merely his customers; but except that their activities are confined, sometimes within the limits of a single district, they are otherwise similar to the big men who live in the cities. More often than not these men take an active and personal part in disseminating drugs, and consequently coming frequently into contact with the authorities, are more often brought to book for their misdemeanours. But they do not have much at stake, and rarely risk more than they can afford to lose if plans go wrong. Of course, there are these men in big cities also; as a matter of fact there are a host of them in every big city. To the square mile, there are many more consumers in a city than in the interior, and as the big smuggler cannot be troubled with retailing minute quantities of drugs, there is plenty to do for the lesser lights.

Why is it that these importers are never brought to book, is a question that might reasonably be asked. The answer is simple. It is because they never by chance handle the goods; they never allow it into their houses. That a certain man is a smuggler is well known to the authorities. In fact, the suspect will cheerfully admit it; he will even go as far as telling them how it was that they failed to seize his last consignment of contraband, and defy them to seize the next one he expects to import! But he is perfectly acquainted with the law, and he knows that he cannot be touched unless the contraband is found in his actual possession, or, under such circumstances, within his house or its precincts, that possession of it cannot be ascribed to anyone but himself. The law prescribes a punishment for any person who, according to general repute, earns his living, wholly or in part, by opium or morphia trafficking. The smuggler evades the first part of this provision by keeping a mercantile business going; and relies upon his personality, and the dread he inspires in those who might otherwise seek to interfere with him, for avoiding the second. The instinctive reluctance of respectable people to make themselves party to judicial proceedings, and a very understandable fear of extremely unpleasant consequences to themselves, deters them from coming forward to give evidence against the smuggler, and this is a great handicap to this very excellent piece of legislation. All that the executive can hope to do is to seize as much of his contraband as possible, and so, gradually, deprive him of the means to carry on his trade.

Smugglers have been reduced to impotence in this way, by repeated seizure of their wares, but their number is not numerous. The weak link in the chain that can be wound round the smuggler is, indubitably, the corrupt preventive officer. It is regrettable, but nevertheless true, that a proportion of the preventive staff is corrupt and amenable to bribes. The smuggler pays them handsomely to keep their eyes closed, and their mouths shut, and being poorly paid by Government the temptation to bribery, which swells their monthly incomes to four or five times what they legitimately earn, is too great to resist. Besides this, many of the men recruited are not of the type most suitable. Their ideals of honesty are nebulous, self-respect to them consists merely in wearing clean clothes. It is a fact that a certain official once appointed his man-servant to the subordinate grade of a preventive department. Rumour had it that this servant was brother to the woman this official was keeping as his mistress, but that was mere scandal, and probably untrue. At the same time, one cannot expect much from a staff which can be recruited in so haphazard a manner. In other walks of life, the need for cautious recruitment is not so vital, and the need to pay for honesty is not so great as in departments whose duty it is to safeguard the revenue, and ensure the moral welfare of the people. It should be made a principle that for every ten rupees paid for actual work, fifty rupees will be paid for its honest performance. The need for this is accentuated in departments in which cupidity, which exists to a greater or less extent in every man, is excited and tempted to the utmost.

Chapter II.

Bribery and Corruption.

No matter how powerful and reckless of consequences a smuggler may be, there is, nevertheless, a lurking respect in his bosom for the myrmidons of the Law. It is to his interest to have the authorities on his side, and, as he cannot have them on other terms, he must pay them handsomely. An excise or police officer, especially if he be of the lower ranks, can make it uncommonly uncomfortable for a smuggler; and it may be taken for granted that a smuggler is not completely satisfied until he has a large proportion of the preventive staff in his pay. To some, however, he will pay nothing because he has nothing to fear from incapables; some who occasionally come in his way he will tip with the economy of the uncle who tips his nephew; but to the able ones, the ones that can make it very warm for him, he will pay handsome monthly salaries, and he will look upon the outlay as money well invested. It is in this way that the smuggler keeps his traffic going; it is thus that he makes it possible to smuggle with profit.

Now, the preventive can only prevent by seizing contraband articles; so that it stands to reason that its efficiency, and the ability of the individuals who compose it, must be judged largely by results; by the number of arrests made, and the quantity of contraband seized. An able officer who makes no hauls may be not unjustly put down as a bribe-taker, and a chief who knows that there is lots of contraband to be seized for the trying, will come down heavily on such a subordinate.

What does the smuggler do when the well-paid watchdog of the Law comes to him and tells him that he will be obliged to seize some, if not all, of the smuggler's next consignment of opium, because the game is, to all intents and purposes, up? Does he wring his hands and roundly curse his ill luck? No; he merely smiles and advises the watchdog to stand at the corner of such-and-such a street, near so-and-so's shop between certain hours next morning, and search the man who passes him with a spotted bandanna round his neck, and a bundle under his right arm. The watchdog acts on the advice, searches the man with the spotted bandanna, finds two cakes of opium, and walks the culprit off to the police station. For this he is commended and paid a reward; the smuggler gets off with the loss of two cakes of opium instead of the hundred he stood to lose; and the man with the spotted bandanna who is ultimately sent to prison for six months, merely fulfils the duty for which he is paid a regular monthly salary.

The foregoing is an example of the methods of smugglers, and of the cupidity of some of the staff employed by Government to guard its revenues. But it is only one. It would weary the reader to be told of the scores of other means employed. The smuggler, knowing that a certain officer is financially embarrassed, will approach him with the offer of a loan, and accept a note of hand for the accommodation. That note of hand releases the smuggler from all further obligation to pay the officer in question. He is well aware that certain dismissal of the latter must result if he shows the scrap of paper in the proper quarter. He has the unfortunate man completely in his hands. But it is obvious that there can be little to fear from a man who provides such damning evidence against himself.

People might well ask how it is that so much corruption can go on and yet no one be caught and punished. Now, it is a well-known principle of evidence that one man's word is as good as another's, and in law, no matter how convincing the truth of a man's story might be, it must usually be corroborated before a magistrate will convict. The giving and receiving of bribes are, by their very nature, secret transactions—transactions to which there are no independent witnesses, so that it is very rarely that the charge can be brought home; and it is usually only those cases in which a confirmed bribe-taker has been lured into a trap, skilfully laid with the aid of marked notes or coins, which have a satisfactory conclusion. It must, moreover, be borne in mind that the giver or offerer of a bribe is just as much liable in law as the receiver or solicitor of it; so that it is seldom that a complaint to a magistrate is made.

The two anecdotes I give here will afford the reader food for thought:

X was a responsible officer. He had the control of a district, and was widely respected. One afternoon, when at office, he had occasion to leave his room, and on his return to it, found ten one-hundred rupee notes under a paperweight on his table. He well knew who had placed them there. He took three of these notes to his superior officer, and with much apparent indignation, handed them to him, and asked that the sum be credited to Government. The guileless superior, ever after thought highly of X's honesty, and reported on him in flattering terms. X became a richer man by seven hundred rupees!

Now for the second story:

Y was one night visited by a smuggler who produced a bag containing five hundred rupees, and offered the money as a bribe. Y stormed at him, and calling in his men, had the smuggler arrested, and sent up for trial on a charge of offering a bribe. The money was produced and counted in court. "How many rupees are there there?" enquired the smuggler. "Five hundred rupees," replied the magistrate. "Oh!" said the rascal, "The bag had a thousand rupees in it when I gave it to the sahib!" And Y was generally regarded as a taker of bribes for the rest of his official life. So does fate sometimes serve the virtuous!

I have given the seamy side of things here. There are, however, many excellent and deserving men in preventive departments—men who would rather stay poor than sell their honour.

Chapter III.

Informers and Information.

Of all those who threaten the smuggler with arrest and loss, the informer is the one he fears most, and accordingly regards with bitter hatred as his greatest foe.

Without information, the hands of the executive are tied; without informers, they would be wholly ineffective; and except for a chance seizure now and then, there would be little for them to do. As things are, the organization of a detective department is so linked up with informers and information that one finds it difficult to conceive of its existing with these eliminated. Detectives of the Sherlock Holmes type exist only in fiction, and although it goes without saying that powers of observation above the ordinary, and an intimate knowledge of men are indispensable in a detective, it is equally indispensable that a detective, as things are, must rely upon information if he wishes successfully to solve any problem of crime.

In writing about informers, I deal mainly with the professional blackguards who make a regular living out of giving information. I do not include those who, to work off a grudge, or who, having seen a crime committed, lodge information in the proper quarter.—I do not look upon these as *informers*. The first is a mean-minded person; the second, one who has a very proper conception of his duty towards society. But the man I deal with is essentially a blackguard, and a very despicable blackguard at that. He has only one object in view when he gives information, and that object is money. He is not burdened with notions of his duty as a citizen. If there was no money to be made out of giving information, he would be the last to go a step out of his way to give any; but he recognizes his value as an important factor in detection, places a price on it, and is paid generously.

I have often been asked by magistrates whether my informers were respectable men. I have felt no hesitation in answering the question emphatically in the negative, and I have no doubt I often set them wondering. But one has only to give the matter a moment's consideration to see how diametrically opposed to all one's notions of fair-play and honour must be the nature and calling of an informer. He must for a time pose as the friend and confidant of his victim, and then turn traitor; and he must bribe, coerce, and wheedle from their allegiance scores of subordinates who would otherwise serve their masters with unswerving loyalty. He is the tempter *in excelsis*; he is unscrupulous in the extreme; he is utterly bad. But for all this, he is, as I have already said, a very necessary link in the chain of detection, and we may, like the pharisee, take comfort in the thought that we are not as other men are—even as these informers! The "*unco gude*" would find a monotonous sameness in their existence if there were none to set-off their unco gudeness!

Nowhere is the need for sharp-witted informers so keenly felt as in departments whose duty it is to prevent smuggling, and it may be taken for granted that the greater the blackguard the fellow is, the more useful he will be, and the more useful an informer is to the executive, the greater danger he goes in of losing his life (because the smuggler does not hesitate as to the means he employs in removing obstacles from his path). The authorities have therefore to consider these things when they come to pay the informer. The legislature also protects him by providing that no officer shall be compelled in a law court to disclose the name of his informer. That advantage is duly taken of this provision there need be no doubt. The officer who gives up the name of his informer has little further information to expect, as the informer very naturally values his life, and will give no information to an indiscreet and injudicious officer.

That the authorities are often imposed upon by informers is a matter of course. There are lots of men in this world who would like to pay off an old score against another, and an easy way to do this is to lodge an information against him. A search of the premises occupied by the suspect results, and although nothing may be found, the attention of the neighbourhood is attracted, and for some time the search is a topic of conversation, which is by no means pleasant for the man whose house is searched. The disgrace attending such an occurrence is intensified if the householder happens to be a man who is respected as upright and honest. Severe punishment is provided by the law for givers of false information, but such cases are happily not numerous.

To take action against an informer for giving false information usually results in deterring genuine informers from giving genuine information; for there are factors which operate against the success of the genuine informer. For instance, the object searched for may be removed just before the search is made, or even during the search, and a blank is drawn. To prosecute the informer for giving false information in such circumstances would be manifestly unjust. If he were prosecuted, other informers would not run the risk of giving information and work would come to a standstill. Where, then, is the line to run? This is a question which confronts the executive with ever-increasing perplexity. It seems to be better to disregard the stray cases of false informing, than to jeopardise the entire preventive department's being. A certain officer, suspecting that a search had been made on false information, issued an order, *ex cathedra*, that all informations should be verified before search was made. As the only way in which information can be verified is by making a search, it is not clear to what extent this order was conceived in a spirit of bumptiousness, and how much of it in ignorance.

"Planting," or the fabrication of false evidence, is a favourite and much practised trick of the informer. By means best known to himself he introduces something incriminating into the house of a person against whom he has a spite, and lays an information. A search is made, the stuff is found, and very often an innocent man is fined or sent to jail. Against this there seems to be no remedy, except the employment of well-known, reliable informers, and also a sort of intuition which develops with experience in officers themselves.

In olden days, when coastguards did not exist, Cornwall was a hot-bed of smuggling, and the temper of the Cornishmen towards informers can be gauged by the following story which has much in it that is apropos:—

The Rev. R. S. Hawker, of the parish of Morwenstowe, relates how on one occasion a predecessor of his presided, as the custom was, at a parish feast, in cassock and bands, and presented, with his white hair and venerable countenance, quite an apostolic aspect and mien. On a sudden, a busy whisper among the farmers at the lower end of the table attracted his notice, interspersed as it was with sundry nods and glances towards himself. At last one bolder than the rest addressed him, and said that they had a great wish to ask his reverence a question, if he would kindly grant them a reply; it was on a religious subject that they had dispute, he said. The bland old gentleman assured them of his readiness to yield them any information in his power, but what was the point in dispute? "Why, sir, we wish to be informed if there are not sins which God Almighty will never forgive?" Surprised, and somewhat shocked, he told them that he trusted there were no transgressions common to themselves, but if repented of and abjured, they might clearly hope to be forgiven. But with natural curiosity, he inquired what sorts of iniquities they contemplated as too vile for pardon. "Why, sir," replied the spokesman, "we thought that if a man should find out where run-goods was deposited, and should inform the Gauger, that such a villain was too bad for mercy!"

Chapter IV.

Some Anecdotes of Smugglers and Smuggling.

As an inducement to seize contraband, Government pays its preventive staff money-rewards which bear a ratio to the value of the stuff seized, and the ability displayed in seizing it; and an officer who is active and conscientious very often can earn in this way from three to four times the amount of his monthly salary. But the seizing of contraband is by no means easy, as the smuggler has brought concealment to a fine art, and there seems to be no end to the ingenuity which may be exercised by him in getting his consignments through safely to their destination. A few examples will serve to demonstrate this.

Vigorous search had failed to bring to light the cocaine which was reported to be on board the S.S. "*Contrebandier*" from Marseilles, and the search party were about to reluctantly abandon their quest when attention was directed to a pile of bundles of planks, each bundle consisting of from four to six half-inch planks, bound together at each end with iron bands. More from curiosity than with any idea of discovering cocaine, one of these bundles was pulled apart. The top plank was found to be intact, and so was the bottom one, but the intervening planks had had spaces cut through them which were packed with one-ounce packets of cocaine. A large quantity of the alkaloid, valued at several thousands of rupees, was found. An illustration to make the method clear is shown.

Another example: The weekly steamer from India had come into a Burma port, and the deck-passengers had been lined up on the pier for inspection by the Customs officers. An excise officer on the pier was made curious by four natives of India, whose only effects consisted of earthen pots of water containing small fishes. Knowing that the place to which these men had come abounded with fish of the best kinds, he was not convinced when they explained that they had brought these small fry to stock the local tanks with. A closer scrutiny disclosed the fact that whereas by percolation the outsides of the pots ought to have been wet, these were quite dry. Measurements taken with his walking stick inside a pot and outside it disagreed too greatly to leave any doubt of the existence of a false bottom, and on breaking a pot, he found that it not only had a false bottom, but that the inter-space was packed with segments of opium. The remaining pots, needless to say, were treated in the same way, and a rich haul was made. An illustration of this method, also, is given. Considering there was no seam, the workmanship of these pots was uncommonly clever.

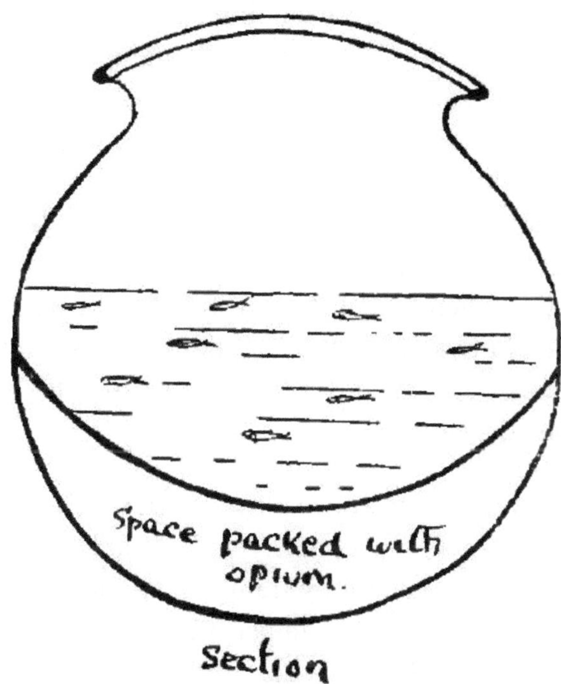

There are doubtless hundreds of other methods as yet undiscovered by which smugglers get their goods through safely. There is the heavy wooden bedstead, whose every leg is hollowed out to receive stuff, whose frame is but a shell to receive morphia phials. It is likely that the Chinaman who walks in front of you wearing a pith hat has cut-out spaces under the padded cover, in the pith, which are occupied by segments of opium; there is the Holy Bible that comes by post, with a square cut in the pages, containing opium or some other drug. The ways in which concealment is practised are legion. The wonder is that so many of these tricks are discovered!

But there are a number of cases in which the methods come to light only after the coup has been completed. A European, Hobson by name, ostensibly a coffee planter, whose plantation was on the frontier which separates an opium-producing country from British India, took to smuggling opium down to city smugglers, and in time accumulated great wealth. His methods were simple, but on one occasion a consignment he had sent down in charge of an assistant of his very nearly fell into the hands of the authorities, and he became more cautious. On one occasion after this, he ordered a consignment of fifty one-pound tins of tea from an oilmanstore merchant in the city, and on its arrival, took delivery. Next day, the same package was returned by rail to the address of the grocer. On arrival of the package in the city, a European, purporting to be an assistant of the grocer firm, called at the railway booking office, and producing the railway receipt, took delivery of the case; the grocer being duly paid, never knew that the package had ever been returned to his address. The explanation is that Mr. Hobson had emptied the tea tins when he got them, refilled them with opium, and sent them back; but the railway receipt was sent to his assistant who, on arrival of the package, took delivery of it, and handed it over to the local smuggler in exchange for hard cash!

How this same Mr. Hobson once played a trick on a prominent detective will bear relating, even as inadequately as I am able to do it. Hobson was once travelling down to the city by train, when our sleuth, who happened to be on tour, entered the same compartment at a small wayside station. Having already seen Mr. Hobson's descriptive roll, he had no difficulty in identifying him as the smuggler whom he had often dreamt about catching; and having the strongest reason to believe that H could not possibly know who *he* was, introduced himself as Mr. Jackson, travelling for a firm of leather merchants. The two got into conversation, and our sleuth, being an adept in the art of worming out details of other people's affairs, soon got Hobson to open his heart to him. Facts and figures were eagerly noted whenever Hobson was not observant of it, and our sleuth was very pleased indeed with himself. Next morning, however, as he parted from his late companion at the city railway station, Hobson said, "Good-bye, Mr. ——" addressing him by his real name, "I am very pleased indeed to have made your acquaintance. Here," producing it from his pocket book, "is your latest photograph! Let me advise you to represent anything but leather another time. You don't know a thing about it." And then, as an afterthought, "Better tear up those notes you took. I've told you nothing that isn't a damned lie!"

An Indian smuggler once took a rise out of a certain high police official, whom I shall call Duncan, and thereby made a mortal enemy for life. F. was the chief smuggler in this city, and his transactions in illicit drugs ran into lakhs of rupees. It was most desirable that this prince of smugglers should be brought to book. He was also by way of being a desperate character; for although it could not be proved, it was morally certain that more than one of the mysterious murders that had taken place in recent years had been committed or instigated by him. One day Duncan got information that F. had a large quantity of drugs, arms, and ammunition in his house, and that if search were made at once, F. would, to a certainty, be caught red-handed. This was luck indeed, and Duncan decided to make the search personally. Collecting a party of constables, he set out at once, but meeting the Black Maria (prison van) on its way back to the prison from the Courts, a brilliant idea came to him, and halting this grim conveyance, he and his party entered it, giving instructions to the driver to stop opposite F.'s house. Arriving there, some of the party soon surrounded the house, while Duncan and the rest of them entered the place. F. was in his "Office," to all appearances deeply immersed in piece-goods transactions.

"F.," said Duncan, "I am going to search your house on information received. I believe you have contraband drugs, arms, and ammunition concealed somewhere on these premises, and I mean to find them. If you wish to search me and my party before we begin, do so at once."

"I am a humble, law-abiding merchant, Sahib, and have no concern with drugs and firearms. You are quite at liberty to search anywhere you please."

The search began. Duncan, although by no means a young man, worked with the rest. The place was ransacked from cellar to attic, but not a trace of what was sought was to be found. Duncan, covered from head to foot in grime and cob-web, at last reluctantly decided to give it up, and slowly descended the stairs to the lower room, where he was struck speechless with indignation. There was a table covered with the whitest of linen cloths, and groaning under an assortment of fruit and sweetmeats, crowned by a bottle of Pommery and Greno; while F., with a snowy towel over his arm, and a silver bowl of water in his hands, greeted Duncan with an invitation to wash and partake of refreshment "as your honour looks tired and dusty."

"Damn you! I shall have you yet," said the infuriated Duncan when he found his tongue; and strode out of the house with rage and hatred in his heart!

It was discovered later that F., in a mischievous mood, had himself forwarded the information on which Duncan acted!

Chapter V.

More Anecdotes.

Bloody encounters with smugglers are rare, but they do happen sometimes, and as it is always on the cards that active opposition may be encountered when a party sets off to intercept a smuggler on his way to "market," the work of an exciseman is not entirely free from danger. Very often when a smuggler goes on a journey, he travels armed with sword or spear; sometimes with a musket; sometimes even with a modern revolver or shot-gun. He is prepared to use these, and unless the intercepting party gets the "drop" on him, he will put up a good fight. Unfortunately, the officer, as a rule, though acquainted to some extent with the law governing the right of private defence of public servants acting in an official capacity, does not take full advantage of it; he has not been bred to kill; and it is probable that there is a lurking fear in him that the magistrate, who will hold the enquiry, will not see quite eye to eye with him, and that he may, perhaps, be convicted of a rash and negligent act, or grievous hurt, if he merely wounds his man, or even, perhaps, of culpable homicide. To some extent he probably is justified in so thinking. Not long ago, an officer fired off his pistol in a melee following on a seizure, and wounded one of his assailants in the arm. A complaint was made, and the unfortunate young officer was convicted of grievous hurt, and sentenced to three months rigorous imprisonment and a fine. It is true he was afterwards retried and acquitted, but he was in no way compensated for the agony of mind he suffered, or for the degradation he had undergone in being tried as an ordinary criminal. This is chiefly to show that there is justification for an officer thinking twice or oftener before he proceeds to take risks. But the general run of magistrates are broad-minded men; men who combine with a sound knowledge of law, worldly wisdom, and a knowledge of the special conditions, and it is extremely rare for a conscientious officer to be "let down." I shall now tell a story based on fact.

Information was brought to the inspector of ... that a certain well-known smuggler was on his way to ... and that he had a large quantity of illicit opium with him. Report had it that he was armed, and, accordingly, the inspector, providing himself with a revolver of small calibre—really nothing more than a toy—and his peon, with a shot-gun loaded with slugs in both barrels, set off with a small party to a certain pass in the hills near by, through which the smuggler would have to pass. In due time the smuggler, with a load on his shoulders, and a Tower musket in his hand, came along.

"Halt," called the inspector, jumping from his place of concealment, and covering the smuggler with his toy revolver.

The only reply was a flash and bang from the smuggler's musket, and for a moment, the air was thick with smoke and nasty whining sounds, as missiles of all kinds flew past the inspector's head.

"Now I will shoot you," said the inspector, and he fired a shot over the smuggler. The smuggler poured some powder down his musket barrel.

"Put down that gun!" ordered the inspector, and he fired another shot over the smuggler's head. Now a piece of wadding clanged down under the smuggler's ramrod.

"I shall certainly shoot you now," threatened the inspector, and another tiny bullet whistled harmlessly past the smuggler. This time a handful of slugs went rattling down the long barrel.

"Can my master be bewitched?" thought the peon, who had the loaded shot-gun in his hands. "It must be so; but matters are getting too serious for further argument," and levelling the gun at the smuggler he fired off both barrels at once, almost cutting the fellow in halves. A large quantity of opium was found in the smuggler's bundle and the judicial officer who held the inquiry, a man who had risen from the bottom of the ladder, and whose experience was wide, while admiring the inspector's humanity, considered that he had no right to expose himself and his party in the way he did. He wanted it to be widely known that smugglers who went armed with the idea of terrorising the executive did so at the risk of being shot at sight, and he undertook to see that officers who did this did not suffer. The peon was handsomely rewarded and promoted for his presence of mind and opportune action.

Here is another story.

I had received information that a certain smuggler of repute expected a big consignment of opium, and that it would reach his house sometime during the night and be concealed there. It was about nine o'clock in the evening when I set out, clad in an old grey suit, cap, and muffler, for the smuggler's house, intending to conceal myself somewhere near, and watch proceedings. As I entered the quarter where the smuggler lived, I was accosted by two beat constables who suggested that I was a member of the crew of one of the tramp steamers then lying in the harbour. After apparently satisfying them of my identity, I continued on my way, and was soon ensconced under a large tree, with the smuggler's house and compound in full view. I had not been there an hour, when I heard the sound of approaching footsteps, and looking round, was not a little annoyed to find the beat constables again on my track. They had spotted me in the gloom of the tree, and being suspicious, had come to see who I was. To me it seemed that there was nothing to be gained after this by continuing the watch, and so, roundly abusing the two inquisitive myrmidons of the law, I went home. I was later to regret my unkindness to my two preservers, for that, indeed, they proved to be. Next morning I was called upon by one of my spies, who handed me a wicked looking dagger with a blade at least five inches long.

"What might this be?" I asked.

"Sahib," he replied, "if it had not been for the two policemen that disturbed your watch last night, that dagger would have taken your life. While you watched, there was one who watched you with this dagger. When the two policemen came along, he dropped the weapon and made off."

No name was given, and it would have done no good to have taken proceedings against my would-be assailant, even if I had known his name. Such things are all in the day's work. But I had the satisfaction the same day of going down to the smuggler's house and unearthing over a maund of his opium. It is true that he got off at the trial on a technical point, but he lost a great deal of money, actually and potentially, and I felt I had called quits to the person who was the instigator of my attempted murder.

Chapter VI.

Observations on Smugglers and Smuggling.

Taken all round, I think it must be admitted that the smuggler is a sportsman, in the sense that he plays a hazardous game at great personal risk, at the risk of his fortune, and against great odds. It is true that he takes all the care he can to minimize risks, but he can never hope entirely to eliminate the element of danger; and if his game be divested of all its peccancy, and most of its immorality, we discover in it the essentials of what goes to make horse-racing so popular a "sport" all over the civilized world. What is it that attracts millions to a race-course? Money! The desire to get money coupled with the excitement of the game. Out of every thousand persons who go to a race-meeting, nine hundred and ninety-nine go to gain money under feverishly exciting conditions, and *one* to see the horses run. Spanish bull-fighting however it may please the Spaniard, can never be otherwise than disgusting to an Englishman. But however shocked an Englishman might be at the ruin the smuggler causes to thousands of his fellow-men, he can never feel for the smuggler the contempt which he feels for the gaudy and bespangled Toreador. He recognizes that the smuggler is playing a dangerous game, sustained by the arts of a subtle intellect, and that he also possesses the qualities which go to make a good fighter.

It may be that the smuggler has little notion of the havoc he spreads. It may be that he argues thus: "There is a demand for drugs, and people will be supplied by some means or other. They are willing to pay almost any price for the drugs they want; they are grown up people and well able to judge for themselves; why should I not make a fortune by supplying them with their wants at my own price?" This is a form of reasoning which contains no fallacy for a man unacquainted with the principles of ethics, and it is certain that the smuggler has not burdened his mind with such learning, admirable as it may be.

His offence against the revenue laws provides the smuggler with a never-ending source of pure delight. Every fresh triumph in this direction he looks upon as another feather in his already innumerably be-feathered cap.

But there can be no question about the dreadful misery for which the smuggler is directly responsible, and in succeeding chapters I shall endeavour to give as realistic a picture as I can of the awful results of this damnable traffic in drugs.

THE DRUG HABIT.

Chapter VII.

Opium.[1]

It may be taken for granted that most people are in some degree acquainted with the use of opium, having had it at some time or other administered to them as a medicine. Dover's powder, so useful a remedy for a cold, contains opium; Laudanum is a preparation of it which is familiar to everybody; and there are scores of other remedies and proprietary preparations which contain opium to a greater or less extent. But useful as opium may be, it must be used with discretion, and must not be allowed to change its character of a faithful servant for that of a master. It can become an exacting and dominating master, and the habit once formed is well nigh ineradicable.

For the information of those who have not seen the pure drug, I may mention that opium is a dark brown, putty-like substance with an agreeable, sweetish, odour. It is the dried resin obtained by incising the unripe capsules of a certain variety of poppy, and is prepared in large, well-equipped factories, from which it is issued in cakes and balls weighing eighty tolas.[2]

The opium industry is a Government monopoly. The poppy crops are grown under Government supervision, and the factories where it is prepared belong to Government and are staffed by Government servants. The prepared product is sold from Government opium shops from which consumers who are so privileged can get their requirements at a certain fixed price.[3] But as

[1] For a full account of the history of opium, see the Appendix at the end of the book.

[2] One tola is equivalent to 180 grains. Eighty tolas equal one *seer*.

[3] Government does not vend opium directly to the people. A selected "licensee"

is the case with all monopolized commodities, opium may assume a money value far in excess of its intrinsic worth and be sold for its weight in silver. In fixing the price of opium, Government is confronted with a choice between two courses: either to sell opium cheap, and so extinguish the smuggler; or to prohibit it entirely and thereby convert India into a happy hunting ground for the avaricious and rapacious fortune hunter. It takes a middle course, therefore, and sells opium at such a rate that facilities for obtaining it are reasonable, without, on the one hand, rendering it cheap and easily obtainable, or, on the other, making it prohibitive. The policy pursued is one of eventual suppression; the discouragement of recruits to the opium habit being the means employed as best adapted to bring about its realization.

The opium habit was an established thing in India centuries before the British first set foot in the country, and it is surmised that it was the Arab conquerors, who invaded India in the 11th century who first introduced it. The cultivation of the poppy, and the preparation of opium, were live industries in India in the 16th century, as Portuguese chroniclers tell us, and when the British East India Company took over the administration of Bengal after Clive's victory at Plassey in 1757, all that they found themselves able to do was to adopt a policy of regulation leading to ultimate suppression. This policy has been followed ever since.

It is a fundamental weakness of human nature that we desire most that which it is most difficult to obtain. It is a perpetuation of the genesiac myth of the forbidden fruit; and no matter how optimistic some may be that the opium habit will eventually be stamped out, it is to be feared that this cannot come about until human nature ceases to be what it always has been. This contention applies with special cogency to the opium habit whose insistence in our midst is not only owing to the fact that it satisfies the sensuousness and voluptuousness which forms a part of every man's nature, but that it establishes a dominance over its victims which requires almost super-human power of will to overthrow. In a letter to his friend and medical attendant Mr. Gilman, Coleridge, who was for twenty-five years a victim to the opium habit, writes about the giving up of it as a "trivial task" and as requiring no more than seven days to accomplish; yet elsewhere he

undertakes this under the supervision of a Government officer, usually an Excise Inspector.

describes it pathetically, and sometimes with almost frantic pathos, as the scourge, the curse, the one almighty blight which had desolated his life. De Quincey very justly calls this a "very shocking contradiction," and asks, "Is, indeed, Leviathan *so* tamed?"

It has been more than once suggested that the dissemination of a healthy propaganda would be the best means of deterring recruits to the opium habit, and that reliance upon the efforts of a strong preventive staff can result only in a diminution of the vice, and not its extinction. On some, such propaganda might have the desired effect; but with others, it may have just that effect which we seek to avoid. There is always a desire to experience new and strange sensations; there are always some who want an unfailing panacea for pain of body or mind; there are always some who long for oblivion. All these things are to be got from opium—the sovereign panacea for pain, grief, "for all human woes"; a weaver of dreams and ecstasies! And so, with the personal equation always solving itself, the problem remains to all intents and purposes unsolvable.

Let us see what the effects of opium are. A writer on the subject says, "A small dose not unfrequently acts as a stimulant: there is a feeling of vigour, a capability of severe exertion, and an endurance of labour without fatigue. A large dose often exerts a calming influence with a dreamy state in which images and ideas pass rapidly before the mind without fatigue, and often in disorder, and without apparent sequence. Time seems to be shortened as one state of consciousness quickly succeeds another, and there is a pleasant feeling of grateful rest. This is succeeded by sleep which, according to the strength of the dose, and the idiosyncrasy of the person, may be light and dreamy, or like normal profound sleep, or deep and heavy, passing into stupor or coma. From this a person may awaken with a feeling of depression, or langour, or wretchedness, often associated with sickness, headache, or vomiting." I have verified these statements by questioning numerous consumers of opium, and, in substance, their descriptions tallied exactly with that I have quoted.

How the opium habit is first contracted is a matter which deserves investigation, but it would seem that the most fertile cause is its injudicious administration in its character of an anodyne. De Quincey, in his "*Confessions of an English Opium-Eater*" tells us that he first took opium for a severe toothache. The poet Coleridge, who, like De Quincey, was a confirmed opium-eater, "began in rheumatic pains"; and if a census of consumers was taken, it would not be surprising to find that eighty *per cent.* of them were first introduced to this "dread agent of unimaginable pleasure and pain" by its being given them for a stomachache, toothache, or some such wrecker of the peace of their mind. The other twenty *per cent.* are the victims of curiosity. The Burman is said to get the taste for opium when he is drugged with it while young, when he is, according to Burmese custom, tattoed from the waist to above his knees.

Nobody needs to be told that a habit is formed by the frequent repetition of acts or indulgences, and that some habits are more difficult to break ourselves of than others. The opium habit falls in this category. It is formed, of course, in the same way as other habits, but there are peculiarities connected with it on which those who are ready to condemn opium-eaters as degenerates might well ponder. The physiological effects of opium are such, that the wearing off of the effects of a dose are attended with the keenest mental and physical distress. No one who has not been an opium-eater can describe these adequately. The need, therefore, for a corrective of this condition becomes what seems an urgent necessity, and the only immediate corrective is "a hair from the dog." A succession of these "hairs"—and a not very long succession—forms the habit. Unlike other habits, it is a habit that cannot be cured without immense strength of will, and a readiness to undergo great suffering: pains in the body, diarrhœa, and a general upset of the mental equilibrium. We see, therefore, that the cause of the habit lies here: *the need for opium to alleviate the pangs caused by opium.*

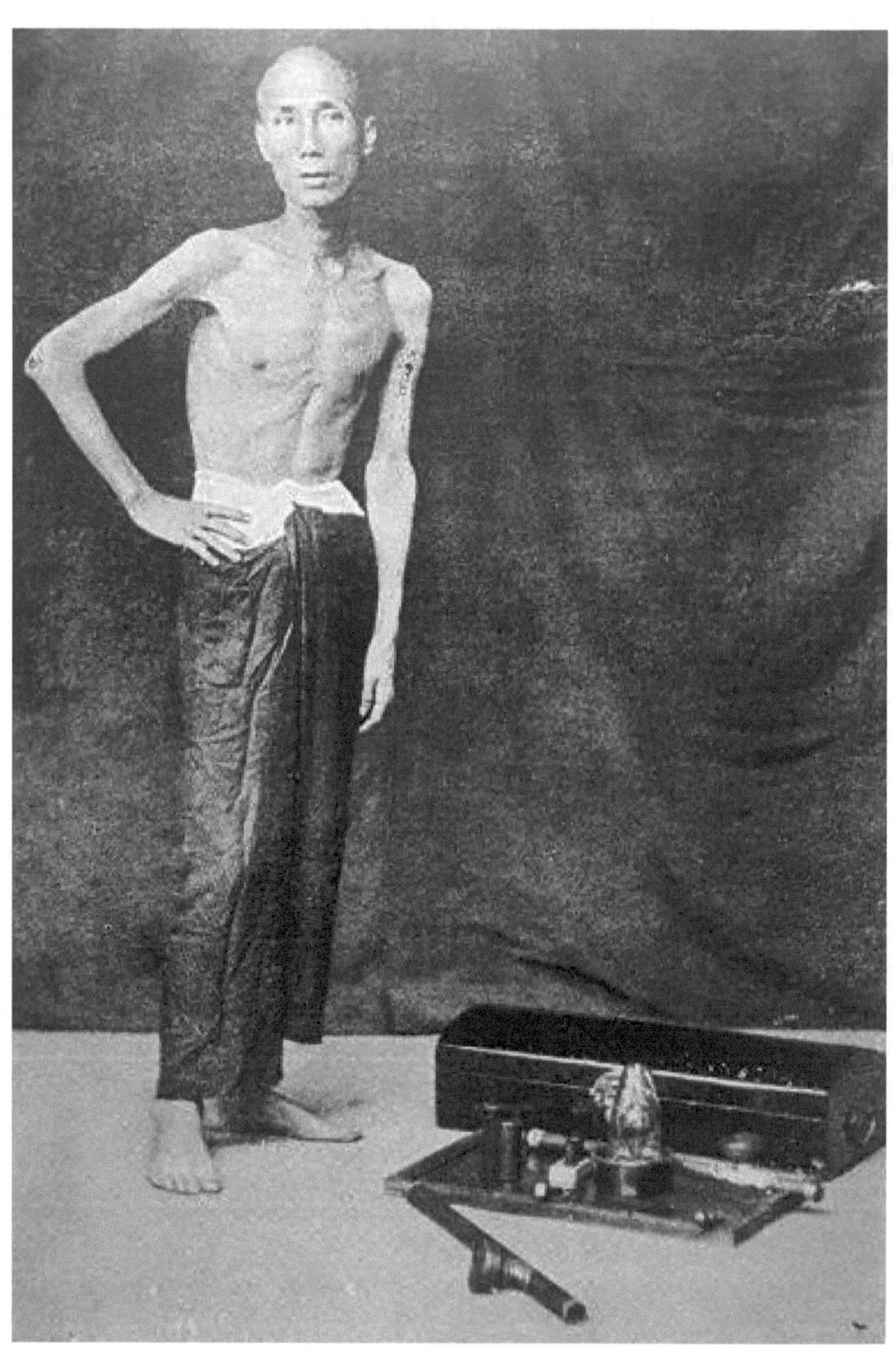

An Excessive Opium Smoker

Amongst unromantically inclined people of the type who form the bulk of consumers—cultivators, coolies, artisans of all kinds, humble folk whose creed is “pice and rice”—it would be difficult (and ludicrous) to suppose that their object in taking opium is to go in their dreams to:

“Woods that wave o’er Delphi steep
Isles, that crown the Aegian deep,
Fields that cool Ilissus’ laves
Or where meander’s amber waves
In lingering lab’rinths creep.”

Possibly, they do have pleasant dreams; but the exertion and hard exercise they must undergo to earn their daily bread is known to counteract the sedative effects of opium; and as they take small quantities only, its effect is to stimulate them rather than to make them dreamy and sensuous; and I contend that, *primâ facie*, it is not to evoke sensuous imaginings that these people take opium. They take it because they cannot get away from it, once the pain to ease which it was given has passed. What strength of will do we expect to find in an unlettered cooly?

* * * * *

Without any apology I reproduce here some verses which appeared in 1894, about the time when the Royal Opium Commission came to India:

THE OPIUM-EATER’S SOLILOQUY.

They began by mourning over my degraded moral state,
Then my physical decadence they would anxiously debate.
Then they raised a pious eye,
And they heaved a pitying sigh,
And they shuddered as they pondered on my melancholy fate.

Now, I never had reflected on the matter thus, at all,
For my luxuries were few, and my expenditure was small.
I was happy as the day,
In my own abandoned way,

Till they said they must release me from the bonds that held me
thrall.

I'd been cheered up at my *Chandoo*[4] shop, for years at least
two score,
To perform my daily labour, and was never sick or sore;
But they said this must not be;
So they passed a stern decree,
And they made my *Chandoo* seller shut his hospitable door.

Now they're sending out Commissions with the philanthropic view
Of inducing us to part with sev'ral crores of revenue;
For all opium traffic's sin,
And, although it brings in tin,
Our nefarious trade papaverous, they say we must eschew.

Who'd have thought that my redemption would have cost so
many lakhs
(For they saddle their expenses on my fellow-subjects' backs).
What with deficits to square,
And Commissions everywhere,
On the "hoarded wealth of India" I shall prove a heavy tax.

If I'd only cultivated, now, a taste for beer or gin,
Or had learnt at Pool or Baccarat my neighbour's coin to win,
I could roam abroad o' nights,
And indulge in these delights,
And my soul would not be stigmatized as being steeped in sin!

But as mine's a heathen weakness for a creature-comfort, far
Less pernicious than their alcohol, more clean than their cigar,
They have sent their howlings forth,
From their platform in the North,
And 'twixt me and my poor pleasures have imposed a righteous
bar!

[4] *Chandoo*, the Indian name for prepared or clarified opium used in smoking. The Burmese name for it is *Beinsi*.

Chapter VIII.

Opium Smoking and Opium-Eating.

There are two modes of taking opium. It is either eaten in its crude form, or it is clarified with water and smoked in a pipe of peculiar construction.

It is generally conceded that opium smoking is less injurious than opium eating, bulk for bulk, of the amount consumed, and that the intemperate or immoderate opium smoker is less liable to the toxic effects of opium than the man who eats it raw. Why this is will be clear when it is explained that as a result of the process of preparation for smoking it, which consists in boiling opium with water, filtering several times, and boiling it down again to a treacly consistency, a considerable portion of the narcotine, caoutchouc, resin, and other deleterious elements are removed, and this prolonged boiling and evaporation have the effect of lessening the amount of alkaloids in the finished product. The only alkaloids likely to remain in the prepared opium, and capable of producing marked physiological effects, are morphia, codeia, and narceia. Morphia in its unmixed state can be sublimed; but codeia and narceia are said not to give a sublimate. But even if not sublimed in the process, morphia would, in the opinion of Mr. Hugh M'Callum (Government Analyst at Hong Kong), be deposited in the bowl of the pipe before the smoke reached the mouth of the smoker. The bitter taste of morphia is not noticeable when smoking opium, and it is therefore possible that the pleasure derived from smoking opium is due to some product formed during combustion. This supposition is rendered probable by the fact that the opium most prized by smokers is not that containing the most morphia.

But what constitutes moderation or the reverse? The answer is idiosyncrasy, or the degree of toleration. This is a factor which is lost sight of by most of those who declaim against the occasional glass or pipe. They wish to push temperance to the point of total abstinence, and condemn the man who takes a peg of whisky without evil results, with the man who becomes maudlin after taking a single glass of white wine, for it is only by outward appearances they are able to judge. But leaving them to rage in their ignorance, we must recognise the fact that opium is one of those drugs the effects of which depend largely upon personal idiosyncrasy and toleration. Dr. Chapman, in his *Elements of Therapeutics*, gives two instances of remarkable cases of toleration of opium. In one, a wineglassful of laudanum was taken by a patient several times in the twenty-four hours; and in another, a case of cancer, the quantity of laudanum was gradually increased to three pints daily, a considerable quantity of crude opium being also taken in the same period!

The usual dose, as a medicine, is from one to three grains of opium, but a consumer can take from ten to twenty, while I have met many able to take from sixty to eighty grains. The degree of tolerance is increased by usage and habit, and the tendency is to increase the dose with habituation. With smokers, it is not uncommon to find Chinamen, the heaviest consumers of opium in the world, who can dispose of three tolas[5] of opium in the day; but they smoke it, and so can stand far more of it than if they ate it in the crude state.

The reader who has troubled to come so far with me will not unreasonably be curious to know how opium is smoked; so, if he will accompany me farther, I will take him into a den and satisfy his curiosity. It is a Chinese den. From the street it has nothing to proclaim its character; it is like any other entrance in the street. Ah! Here comes a smoker. Observe his deathly pallor, his appearance of emaciation, his dazed expression. He must be a heavy smoker, soaked in the vice. Let us go in with him! We enter. For a moment the dimness of the room flanked on three sides with raised wooden

[5] Three tolas is 540 grains, or 1½ oz.

platforms waist-high, and covered with mats, is accentuated by our sudden entrance from the sunlit street. We become aware of a peculiar odour in the atmosphere of the room, not unpleasant, but peculiar. It is like nothing that we have ever sniffed before. It is the odour of smoked opium. When our eyes, having got used to the light, or rather darkness, of the room, we look round and see on the platforms, sleeping forms sprawled round trays containing their smoking utensils. Let us examine these: First there is the pipe. It is made of a single joint of bamboo about a foot and a half long, hollow, and closed at one end, and about an inch in diameter. About a quarter of its length up from the closed end, there is an earthenware protuberance, not unlike a door-knob in appearance, firmly fixed into the stem; on its top, and in the centre, is a small orifice. This is the pipe-bowl.

Next we notice a lamp. This has a base of wood, and consists of a glass reservoir of oil, with a string wick leading from it through a small brass cap. Over this is a glass chimney.

Then we see the wire, like an ordinary fine knitting needle; and several horn phials, each containing prepared opium.

But here is the new-comer whom we followed in. He has paid the den-keeper the small fee which makes him the temporary owner of a tray of smoking utensils, and with these he passes us, and getting on to the platform between two sleepers, he puts his tray down, and assumes a recumbent attitude beside it. Lying on his left side, with his head on a hard lacquered pillow, he draws the tray towards him and takes the pipe in his left hand. With the other hand he takes the piece of wire, and plunges one end of it into the horn phial containing treacly prepared opium, withdrawing it immediately with a drop of the fluid adhering to the point. This he maintains on the point by rapidly twirling the instrument between two fingers, and carrying it over the flame of the lamp, he proceeds to roast the opium. This is a delicate operation, and requires practice. The needle is dipped into the phial again and again, and the opium adhering to the end roasted over the flame until an appreciable quantity of the drug has accumulated on the end of the wire.

Opium Smokers' Appliances

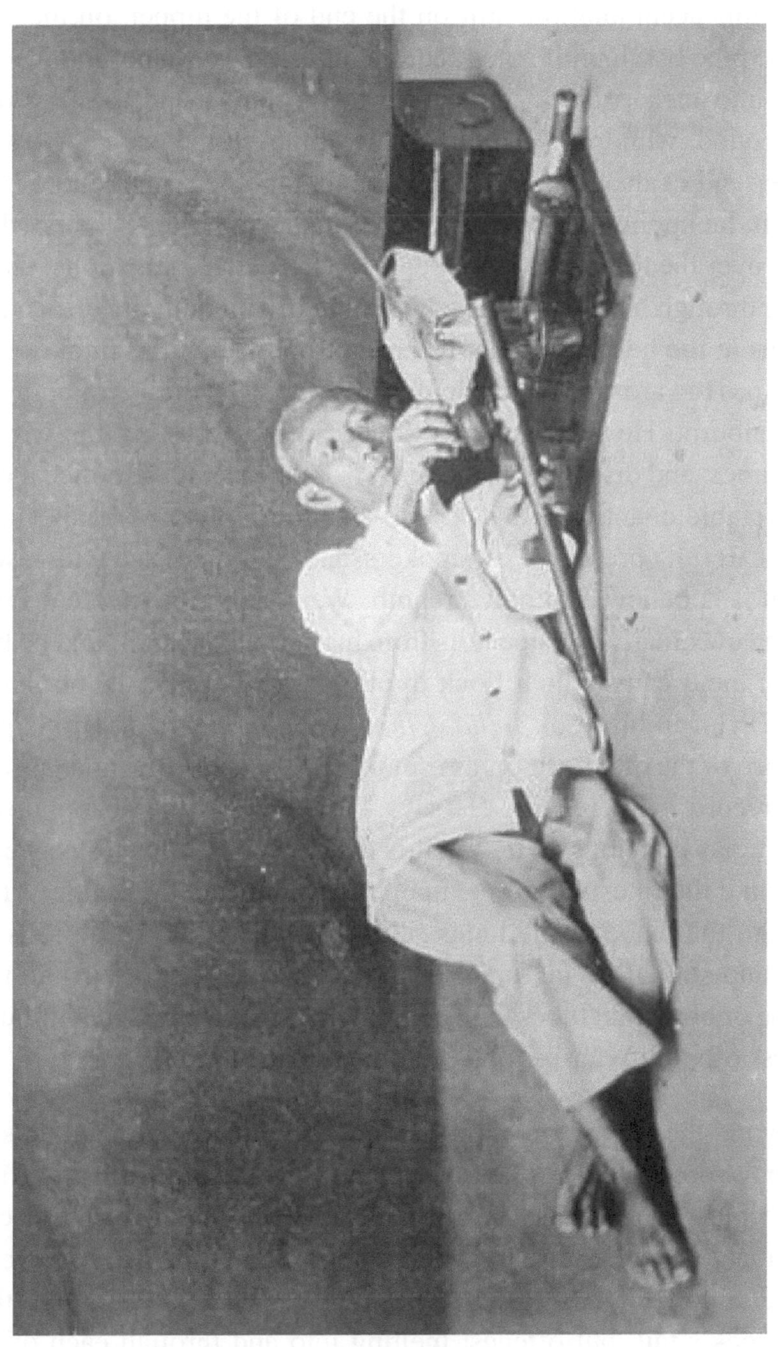

Preparing to Smoke Opium

(*The opium on the end of the dipper being roasted over the lamp.*)

He rolls this accumulation, still on the end of the dipper, on the flattened top of the pipe bowl, until it has acquired the desired shape, and then thrusts the end into the orifice in the centre of the bowl, and twirling the wire sharply round, withdraws it, leaving the opium in the orifice. Now, taking the lower end of the pipe in his right hand, and the mouth end of the pipe in his left, he applies the open end to his lips and holding the bowl almost inverted over the top of the lamp begins to take long inhalations, the smoke escaping through his nostrils. The little plug of opium in the orifice crackles and burns in the heat of the flame, and we notice that the smoker now and then scrapes towards the orifice in the bowl, all the particles of opium which remain unburnt. He finally clears the orifice by thrusting the wire into it several times, and disconnects the bowl from the stem. We notice it contains an appreciable quantity of black, evil-smelling opium residue. This is the "dross," carefully preserved by smokers, and later on boiled with raw opium to which it is believed to add strength. We watch him smoke a few more pipes, and eventually the pipe falls from his nerveless hands, and he lies still. What are the dreams which flock through his mind? We do not know, but Bayard Taylor in his book *India, China and Japan* tells us of his personal experience of the effects of opium smoking. It was his first and last attempt, and his record is interesting. He says:—"To my surprise I found the taste of the drug as delicious as its smell is disagreeable. It leaves a sweet, rich, flavour, like the finest liquorice, upon the palate, and the gentle stimulus it conveys to the blood in the lungs fills the whole body with a sensation of warmth and strength. The fumes of the opium are no more irritating to the windpipe or bronchial tubes than common air, while they seem imbued with a richness of vitality far beyond our diluted oxygen.

"Beyond the feeling of warmth, vigour, and increased vitality, softened by a happy consciousness of repose, there was no effect until after finishing the sixth pipe. My spirits then became joyously excited with a constant disposition to laugh; brilliant colours floated before my eyes, but in a confused and cloudy way, sometimes converging into spots like the eyes in a peacock's tail, but oftenest melting into and through each other, like the hues of changeable silk. Had the physical excitement been greater, they would have taken form and substance, but after smoking *nine* pipes I desisted, through fear of subjecting myself to some unpleasant after-effects. Our Chinese host informed me that he was obliged to take twenty pipes in order to elevate his mind to the pitch of perfect happiness. I went home feeling rather giddy, and became so drowsy, with slight qualms at the stomach, that I went to bed at an early hour—after a deep and refreshing sleep, I arose at sunrise, feeling stronger and brighter than I had done for weeks past."

Chinaman Smoking Opium

Chapter IX.

Some Observations on the Opium Habit.

It is now proper that we should ask the question "Is opium the very dreadful thing it is made out to be?" My answer is, yes and no. Anything immoderately indulged in is bad for one. Over-eating, excess in smoking and drinking, are all bad. There is such a thing as too much of even a good thing. I am prepared to admit that excess in opium is worse than most things; but as a choice between opium and drink, I consider drunkenness to be the greater evil. It may be that it is more common, and therefore responsible for more distress in the world than opium; but opium does not, and can never, degrade as drink does, and a man does not make a beast of himself with opium. It does not make a nuisance of a man; it does not lead to violence and to murder as drink does. I do not ask reformers to subscribe to this view. I express it as my own opinion, founded as it is upon close acquaintance with numerous opium consumers, and many drunkards.

What is it that reformers have to urge against opium? They will not admit that opium in moderation does no great harm; they will not agree that the degree of toleration varies in people. Let us take their contentions *seriatim*, and see how they will stand against logical and informed discussion:

They say: (1) That opium in any degree induces physical degeneration.

I say, I have met men of wretched physique who are opium consumers, and men of wretched physique who are not opium consumers. Also, I have met giants in strength who are not opium consumers, and giants in strength who are confirmed opium consumers. I will also say this, that among the hard-working class of Indians and Burmans, such as coolies and porters, the proportion of consumers to non-consumers is about equal, but I have been able to observe no inferiority in capacity in the consumers, and very often have found them superior. Those who wish to learn what the powers of bodily endurance of an opium consumer may be are recommended to read that very readable book "*An Australian in China.*"

(2) That the consumer is mentally inferior to his non-consuming brother.

This I qualify. It depends on the degree of indulgence, and unless this is considered, it is not possible to argue. It is a proved fact that the effect of opium is to quicken the perceptions, and stimulate the imagination. Too often this is taken to be evanescent; and it is assumed that the intellect weakens, and that, eventually, it is enfeebled beyond chance of recovery. But if opium were not taken; in such a case, would not advancing years bring about a like condition? Charles Lamb, who drank more than was good for him, and Coleridge, who was an opium-eater, complained that the effect of their particular "poisons" was to deprive them of their capacity for singing when they awoke in the morning! Lamb complained of this when he was forty-five, and Coleridge at the age of sixty-three. Does anyone imagine they would have been able to "revive the vivacities of thirty-five" if they had been always temperate men?

There is no doubt that, taken in large quantities, opium induces a sluggishness, a lethargy, a stupor; but does not an unusually heavy meal induce a torpor which is incompatible with any sort of intellectual labour? I hold only with moderation.

(3) That indulgence in opium weakens the character and morals.

This applies with equal force to immoderation in most things. It does not hold good of opium taken in moderation. To affirm this is a clear indication of ignorance of the subject. Why, in the name of all that is extraordinary, should a moderate dose of opium make a man a thief, or a criminal, or a moral imbecile? Indians and Burmans, whose religion forbids all manner of intoxicants, condemn their opium-eating brothers to a sort of social ostracism, and when asked for a reason, say, "It is against our religious tenets; and it is very bad in every way." Such uninformed statements are excusable in the unenlightened, but what of those who ought to know, and who pride themselves upon their education and reasoning faculties? They are as clamorous against opium and other things in a more censurable ignorance of facts. Some who will not clear their minds of cant, declaim against a glass of wine with all the fervour and denunciation of fanatics, without rhyme, reason, or apprehension of what they are talking about. In their more fluent and exuberant way, when pressed for a reason, they tell us in effect that indulgence in opium is "Against our religious tenets, and it is very bad in every way." It is time reformers recognised that opium is not such a dreadful thing after all, and confined their attention, and devoted some of their ample leisure, to winning back those who have gone over the limit of moderation, instead of anathematizing them.

It is a pity that reformers do not pursue their propaganda along reasonable and obvious lines, because they would have more supporters and helpers if they did. To publish fulminatory pamphlets against the opium evil, without having any experience of it at first hand beyond an occasional hurried visit to an opium den, is worse than futile; and they cannot hope to convince those who are really in a position, and qualified to help them in their efforts. This is due to a profound ignorance of facts, and a lot of people in India are responsible for the dissemination of a lot of ill-digested nonsense. An enthusiast visits an opium den and finds half a dozen Chinamen sprawled around, with as many opium pipes. He does not know that these men have come in from a ten-hour day's work. He throws up his hands in pious consternation, and writes home about the dreadful place he has visited, and of the horrors of intoxication he witnessed there. The vividness of his description is modified only by the amount of rhetoric at his command, and no one who has come into contact with this sort of person will deny that he always has a vast store!

I once met a missionary, and in the course of conversation, we happened upon the opium evil. He was eloquent, his views on the subject were decided. In fact he was so decided in his views that I found it impossible to convince him that what he described as the effects of opium were really those symptomatic of an overdose of *bhang*. And yet, I have little doubt that this person must have written home lurid accounts of the opium evil, and the ruin and havoc it was causing. What reformers ought to do is to cease memorializing Government to totally prohibit the traffic, and try to help them more by taking an active part in checking immoderation. Moderate indulgence in opium is less harmful in every way than the habit of passing public resolutions and submitting memorials.

By the foregoing, I do not wish it to be surmised that I hold a brief for the opium habit, or that I consider it a desirable thing. To be a slave in any degree to anything is bad; the tobacco habit is bad; the over-eating habit is bad. But opium comes in for too much of the attention of religious propagandists, and the Government is taxed with the charge of reaping revenue at the expense of the bodies and souls of the people. This is a view it is the duty of anyone who knows the subject intimately to correct. The Royal Commission on Opium in India, which sat under the chairmanship of Lord Brassey, some thirty years ago, collected a mass of evidence for and against opium which is unrivalled in its extent and value. The conclusion come to by a majority of the Commissioners was that opium in moderation did no great harm; and to ensure moderation, they recommended a policy of close control. In deference to popular opinion, and the religious scruples of the bulk of Indians, they thought it desirable that the opium habit should eventually be suppressed, and trusted that close control would, by attrition, bring about this result.

Chapter X.

Morphia.

Morphia, which is the active principle of opium, is interesting in its being the first "alkaloid" to be discovered. Its basic nature was first noticed by Serturner in 1816.

As a medicine, principally as an anodyne, morphia is to pharmacy what chloroform is to surgery, and, as a "boon and blessing" to man in that character, it is second to none. But like all good things in this world, it has become the object of the grossest abuse at the hand of man; and its devotees, in an euphonic sense, number hundreds of thousands.

Morphia is a narcotic; that is, it "has the power to produce lethargy or stupor which may pass into a state of profound coma or unconsciousness, along with complete paralysis, terminating in death." The degree of insensibility depends upon the strength of the dose; one-sixth of a grain for an adult man, and one-tenth of a grain for an adult woman, being the largest safe dose given hypodermically. Two or three grains given by the stomach is dangerous. But, as with opium, the dose varies with idiosyncrasy, and some can tolerate larger doses than others. With habituation, some persons can take with impunity an amount of morphia which would prove fatal to five or six healthy, full-grown men. To have its full effect as an hypnotic or anodyne—and its power as the one depends upon its potency as the other—morphia must be given hypodermically.

Group of Morphia-Injectors

The possession of morphia by people other than medical men and chemists is prohibited by law; and the rules governing its sale by chemists are rigid and exact. They must account for every grain sold, and all entries in their sales registers must be supported by prescriptions signed by qualified medical men. Yet morphia injecting is more prevalent in cities than the public is aware of; and it does not require a very penetrating mind to discover that the morphia used by its unfortunate victims comes from illicit sources—from the smuggler. There are, of course, unscrupulous physicians, dentists, and quacks, who pander to the cravings of some of their "patients" by administering regular injections; but we are dealing here with the type of persons who do not call in doctors, accommodating or otherwise. The ones I write about are catered for by an organization which, in spite of the greatest efforts, has been found to be unrepressible.

How do these people get their supplies? Let us go into a morphia den unofficially, and take a glance at it in all its sordidity. We draw aside a filthy sheet of cloth which does service as a curtain, and enter a room about twenty feet square. It is dim almost to darkness; but at the farther end, opposite the entrance door, we notice a wooden partition which has a locked door in it, and near it a hole not unlike the window of a box or ticket office. Through this hole a light is seen, so we presume that there is someone behind the locked door in the partitioned-off portion of the room. Looking round us, we see a row of human figures, clad in the foulest rags, lying along the two sides of the room, near the walls. Some are apparently asleep; actually, they are drugged, overcome by the last injection of morphia. Others are about to make themselves comfortable for a sleep, having just had an injection; while some, too poor to afford the cost of another dose, are groaning and whimpering with the combined agonies of some painful disease, and the wearing off of the effects of the last injection. These accost everybody that enters the den for the price of "just one little injection." They appeal to those who have endured the same pangs with which these unfortunates are wracked. The appeal is to a real, live sympathy; and if it can be spared, the required money is handed over.

One of these beings has not appealed in vain to a fellow votary who has just entered the den in company with two companions, and the four make their way to the hole in the partition, and in exchange for the coppers handed in, a skinny hand passes out four little paper packets, each one containing a dose of morphia powder. Let us peep through the hole, and look at the owner of the skinny hand before following the four to the place to which they have retired. It is a Chinaman, characteristically lean, sitting at a rough table on which is a cigar box filled with paper packets similar to those we saw being handed to the late purchasers. The red and green ones contain morphia, the white cocaine (for he caters for both classes, the injecters of morphia, and eaters of cocaine). Looking up at the hole, he sees us, and thinking we are either excise or police officers, he hastily gathers up his wares, and rushing to the sanitary arrangement in the corner of his cubicle, empties them into the receptacle, and pulling the chain, flushes away the incriminating evidences of his occupation. Being assured that they are well on their way to the sea through the sewer, he turns towards us with a "smile that is child-like and bland," and explains that he has "got nothing—all gone—you can't do nothing." We explain that we had no intention of doing anything, and were merely curious. Recollecting that he had heard no call from his ever watchful colleague who stands by to give timely warning in the event of a raiding party coming in sight, he admits that he has been precipitate; but in no way disconcerted, he sends his colleague off to some place best known to themselves, for a fresh supply of packets.

We now return to the four men who provided themselves with morphia two or three minutes ago. We find them sitting in a ring round another fellow who we learn is the operator. He possesses a hypodermic syringe. Let us take and examine it. It is not the sort of thing one would expect to find in a chemist's show-case or a medical man's pocket-case. This is a weird instrument; the barrel a length of glass tubing; the plunger a bit of knitting needle, whose plunging head consists of tightly wound rag, and whose other end is topped with a conglomerate of sealing wax and sewing thimble. Both joints are lumps of sealing wax, through the lower of which an inch and a half of hollow needle projects. Handing back this septic instrument to the operator, who, by the way, tells us that he gets a copper for every injection he gives, he proceeds to empty the contents of the packets into a small china egg-cup. Adding a modicum of water, and stirring the mixture until a clear solution is formed, he takes up some in the syringe, and one of the expectant waiters draws nearer him. A search is made by the operator for a clear spot on the body of the man, where a dirty needle has not already penetrated and caused a foul sore, and after some search such a spot is found, *on the palm of the hand*, and here the needle is introduced, and the contents of the syringe discharged, after which the man operated on limps away to his place, and lying down, is soon asleep. The next draws near, and having received his share of the dose with the same needle, unsterilized and unwashed, he in turn limps off; and so with the others.

Let us hope that the fell, loathesome, unnameable disease, from which one at any rate of the four was too apparently suffering, has not been introduced into the blood of the others by that death-dealing needle! But it is a hope that we cannot think is justified; the means of propagation employed are too certain to admit of any hope!

The foul and fetid atmosphere of the crowded room is almost overpowering, in spite of the strong tobacco we smoke in our well-lit pipes, but we will linger a little longer and take a glance at those who are lying around like so many logs. Look at this one of them. What an object lesson he is to impetuous youth! Thin to emaciation; his hair fallen off in tufts; his nose almost eaten away; his body covered with sores and ulcers. There is nothing to wonder at in this being taking morphia to ease his pain of mind and body. Since death will not come, let him have oblivion. It is better so.

Here we find a woman; she is a slattern if ever there was one. Clean-limbed, in the sense that she has no sores on visible parts of her body, she is nevertheless almost as certain a disseminator of disease and misery as the foul needle. She wakes as we watch her, and in a drowsy way, smiles; probably in a way she means to be fascinating, but we are not under the effects of the delusive narcotic, so cannot be expected to know! Suddenly a look of intelligence comes into her eyes, and realising who we are, she gets up, and stumbles towards the door, and out on to the street—on her way to *another* den in all probability!

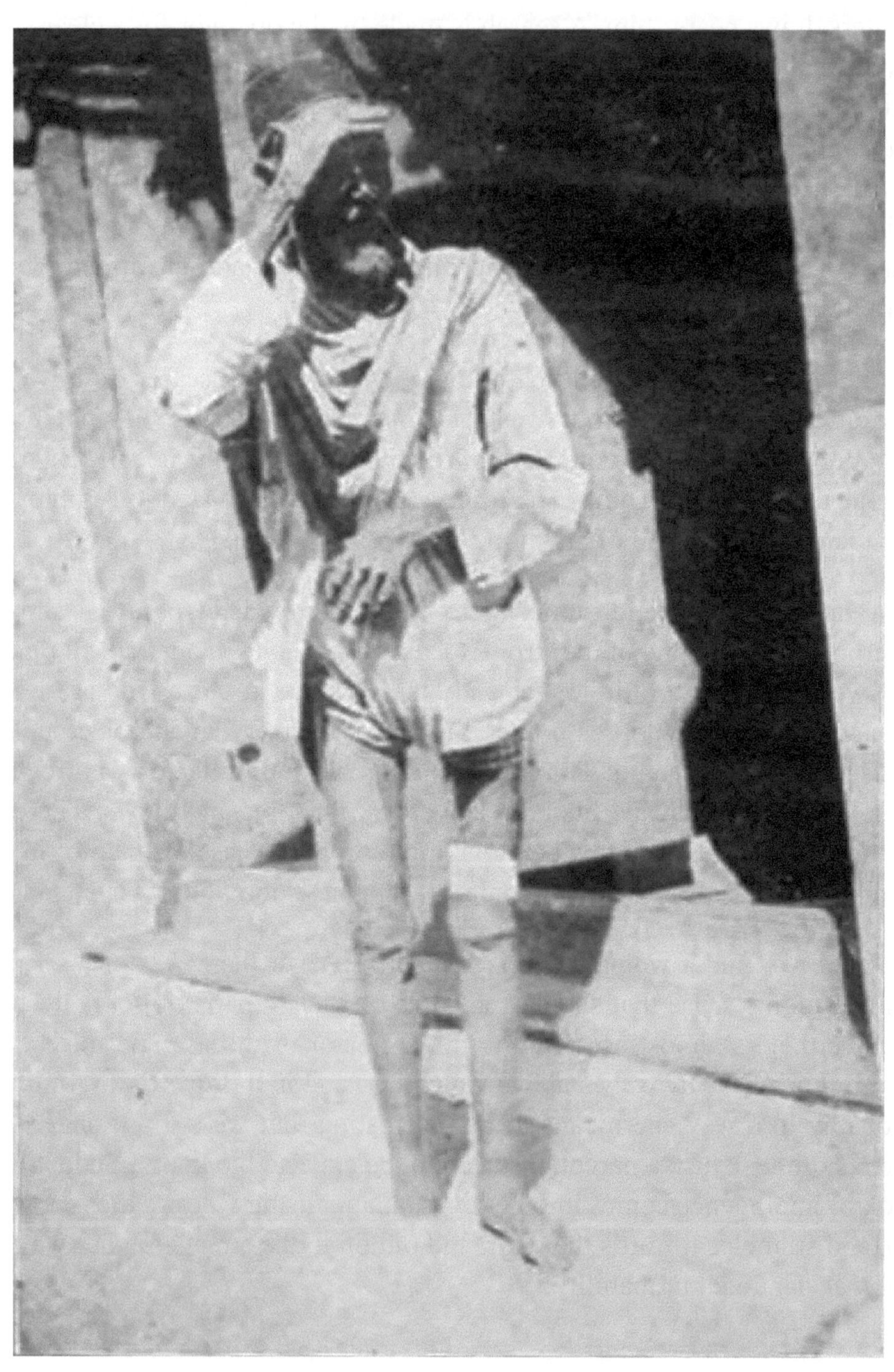

An Indian Morphinist

Here is another. An old, or rather, an old-looking man, shrivelled and feeble. He is just awaking from his stupor. We ask him to get up, but he is unable to do more than humbly indicate the reason for his inability to do so. A glance, as the sheet which covers him is withdrawn from his body, sends a thrill of horror through us, and we turn away sickened at the sight; and the man—is he a man?—draws his cloth over his tattered body, and tries to woo sleep again. This last sight is enough to send us headlong into the fresh air and sunlight. If these are the results of morphia, then God have mercy upon its votaries, for they stand sorely in need of it!

Morphia is imported into the country in large quantities by smugglers, the drug being brought from the British Isles, Japan, and the Continent by members of the crews of steamers plying from these countries. As many as 500 ounces of morphia have been seized in one consignment, and, as it is generally admitted by those who are in position to know that for every ounce seized, a pound passes through undetected, it only requires a simple calculation to arrive at the approximate total quantity which is hawked about unrestricted.

Morphia, being more portable and concentrated, is more easily concealed than opium, which is comparatively bulky. Of the aggregate seizures in any one year, seventy-five per cent. is made up of numerous small seizures. To seize four or five ounces of the drug in one lot is rather the exception than the rule; and seizure in larger quantities is a comparatively rare event.

But it is comforting, in a way, to know that morphia, by the time it reaches the consumer, is very often freely adulterated, starch being the adulterant used; and when it is considered that morphia sold illicitly fetches from five to six times its price when sold licitly, the increase in its bulk which results after adulteration represents a handsome additional profit to the vendor. The big smuggler imports the drug; his lesser brother buys some from him and adulterates it; the den-owner buys the mixture from the lesser light and he in turn adds a little more starch to it; and finally "the man in the cubicle" retails the mixture to the consumer.

There is little to be said in defence of the morphia habit. It is bad, utterly bad, in itself, while it is a fertile disseminator of disease when injected as it is. Morphia ruins a man, body and soul. As is the case with opium, pain is a frequent originator of the habit, but its hold upon the individual is, if anything, stronger than that exerted by opium, and fatal consequences ensue with great certainty and rapidity.

Chapter XI.

Cocaine.

In writing about cocaine, we find that interest lies not so much in itself as in the plant of which it is the alkaloid, the "*erythroxylon coca.*"

The coca plant is indigenous to Peru, and from the most ancient times, Peruvian Indians have chewed the leaves as a habit, as Indians in this country chew the betel leaf and tobacco. "The local consumption of coca is immense," says Dr. Hartwig, "as the Peruvian Indian reckons its habitual use among the prime necessaries of life, and is never seen without a leathern pouch filled with a provision of the leaves, and containing besides a small box of powdered, unslaked lime. At least three times a day he rests from his work to chew his indispensable coca. Carefully taking a few leaves out of the bag, and removing their midribs, he first masticates them in the shape of a small ball, which is called an acullico; then repeatedly inserting a thin piece of moistened wood like a tooth-pick into the box of unslaked lime, he introduces the powder which remains attached to it into the acullico until the latter has acquired the requisite flavour. The saliva, which is abundantly secreted while chewing the pungent mixture, is mostly swallowed along with the green juice of the plant.

"When the acullico is exhausted, another is immediately prepared, for one seldom suffices. The corrosive sharpness of the unslaked lime requires some caution, and an unskilled coca chewer runs the risk of burning his lips, as, for instance, the celebrated traveller Tschudi, who, by the advice of his muleteer, while crossing the high mountain-passes of the Andes, attempted to make an acullico, and instead of strengthening himself as he expected, merely added excruciating pain to the fatigues of the journey."

The poet Cowley succinctly describes the physical effects of coca in the following lines:

"Our Varicocha first this coca sent,
"Endow'd with leaves of wondrous nourishment,
"Whose juice succ'd in, and to the stomach tak'n
"Long hunger and long labour can sustain
"From which our faint and weary bodies find
"More succour, more they clear the drooping mind,
"Than can your *Bacchus* and your *Ceres* join'd.
"Three leaves supply for six days' march afford
"The Quitoita with this provision stor'd
"Can pass the vast and cloudy Andes o'er."

"It is a remarkable fact," Dr. Hartwig tells us, "that the Indians, who regularly use coca, require but little food, and when the dose is augmented, are able to undergo the greatest fatigues without tasting almost anything else." Professor Pöppig ascribes this astonishing endurance to a momentary excitement which must necessarily be succeeded by a corresponding collapse, and therefore considers the use of coca absolutely hurtful. Tschudi, however, is of opinion that its moderate consumption, far from being injurious, is, on the contrary, extremely wholesome, and cites the examples of several Indians who, never allowing a day to pass without chewing their coca, "attained the truly patriarchal age of one hundred and thirty years."

The effects of excess in coca chewing are given by Hill in his *Travels in Peru and Mexico*. "The worst that can be said of the coca is its effects upon the health of such of the Indians as use it in excess. It then affects the breath, pales the lips and gums, and leaves a black mark on either side of the mouth. Moreover, after some time, the nerves of the consumer become affected, and a general langour is said to give plain evidence of the sad consequences of excess."

Another writer gives a more depressing picture of the excessive consumer: "The confirmed coca chewer, or Coquero, is known at once by his uncertain step, his sallow complexion, his hollow, lack-lustre black-rimmed eyes, deeply sunk in the head, his trembling lips, his incoherent speech, and his stolid apathy. His character is irresolute, suspicious, and false; in the prime of life he has all the appearances of senility, and in later years sinks into complete idiocy. Avoiding the society of man, he seeks the dark forest, or some solitary ruin, and there, for days together, indulges in his pernicious habit. While under the influence of coca, his excited fancy riots in the strangest visions, now revelling in pictures of ideal beauty, and then haunted by dreadful apparitions. Secure from intrusion he crouches in an obscure corner, his eyes immovably fixed upon one spot; and the almost automatic motion of the hand raising the coca to the mouth, and its mechanical chewing, are the only signs of consciousness which he exhibits. Sometimes a deep groan escapes from his breast, most likely when the dismal solitude around him inspires his imagination with some terrific vision, which he is as little able to banish, as voluntarily to dismiss his dreams of ideal felicity. How the Coquero finally awakens from his trance, Tschudi was never able to ascertain, though most likely the complete exhaustion of his supply at length forces him to return to his miserable hut."

The coca plant has from ancient times been the object of religious veneration by the Peruvian Indians, and although we have no historical record to tell us when the use of coca was introduced, or who first discovered its peculiar properties, we learn that when Pizarro destroyed Athualpa's Empire, he found that the Incas employed coca in their religious ceremonies and sacrifices "either for fumigation, or as an offering to the gods. The priests chewed coca while performing their rites, and the favour of the invisible powers was only to be obtained by a present of these highly valued leaves. No work begun without coca could come to a happy termination, and divine honours were paid to the shrub itself."

"After a period of more than three centuries, Christianity has not yet been able to eradicate these deeply-rooted superstitious feelings, and everywhere the traveller still meets with traces of the ancient belief in its mysterious powers. To the present day the miners of Cerro de Pasco throw chewed coca against the hard veins of the ore, and affirm that they can then be more easily worked—a custom transmitted to them from their forefathers who were fully persuaded that the Coyas, or subterranean divinities, rendered the mountains impenetrable, unless previously propitiated by an offering of coca. Even now the Indians put coca into the mouths of their dead, to ensure them a welcome on their passage to another world; and whenever they find one of their ancestral mummies, they never fail to offer it some of the leaves."

It is believed that the superstitions regarding coca were looked upon with great disgust by the Spaniards, and that their efforts to stamp them out did more to keep alive the enmity borne them by the Indians than anything else.

The coca plant was first grown in Ceylon in 1870 when it was introduced from Kew. It was grown there as a result of a suggestion made by Mr. Joseph Stevenson who pointed out the commercial importance of the plant in view of the separation of the alkaloid cocaine by Nieman in 1859; but owing to the liability of the coca leaves to rapid deterioration after picking in unfavourable climatic conditions, this branch of commerce has not developed, and as yet no attempt has been made to extract the alkaloid in India, in commercial quantities at any rate.

But no matter what might be said about coca-chewing, there can be no two opinions about the dire and destructive effects of cocaine the alkaloid, and the results of indulgence in this drug are truly deplorable. It may be owing to something else in the coca leaves which ameliorates the full effect of the alkaloid; in fact it must be so, because I doubt whether even a confirmed cocaine consumer could find anything to say in its favour.

The first notice of cocaine consuming appears to be that of Col. J. Watson, who wrote in the *New York Tribune* about cocaine-sniffing. He writes: "I have visited some of the Negro bar-rooms in Atlanta, and the proprietors told me that the cocaine-habit which had been acquired by the Negroes, was simply driving them out of business. When the cocaine-habit fixes itself on a person, the desire for liquor is gone, the victim finding entire satisfaction in sniffing cocaine. By sniffing cocaine up the nostrils it reaches the brain quicker, and the effect is more lasting than if swallowed or administered by hypodermic injection. Persons addicted to the habit say they have tried the two latter ways, and that the effects are not the same, nor do they afford the same degree of satisfaction and pleasure as when sniffed. Unquestionably the drug rapidly affects the brain, and the result has been that, in the south, the asylums for the insane are overflowing with the unfortunate victims. After a person has habitually used the poison for a certain length of time, he becomes mentally irresponsible. No man can use it long and retain his normal mental condition. It is a brain-wrecker of the worst kind."

Cocaine is a highly poisonous narcotic, and when rubbed on the skin, or injected under it, deadens the surrounding parts, and renders them insensible to pain. It is therefore much used in minor surgery, and in ophthalmic and dental operations. As such, it replaces chloroform to some extent. But, unfortunately, its highly stimulating effects, and its power to allay hunger, have been taken advantage of by many thousands of people who have made a habit of taking it, and Col. Watson's description of the dire results of cocaine-sniffing apply with equal force to those which supervene on cocaine-injecting and cocaine-eating, vices that have spread with alarming rapidity all over the civilized world.

The cocaine-habit is an unmixed vice. There is no excuse for it; not even the excuse that the opium and morphia habits have, *viz.*, accident; and the person who takes to it, does so wilfully and deliberately. Cocaine has a greater power over its votaries than either opium or morphia; the after distress is keener; and a slave to it is a slave indeed. And the harm it does, and the certainty with which it eventually kills, is truly appalling.

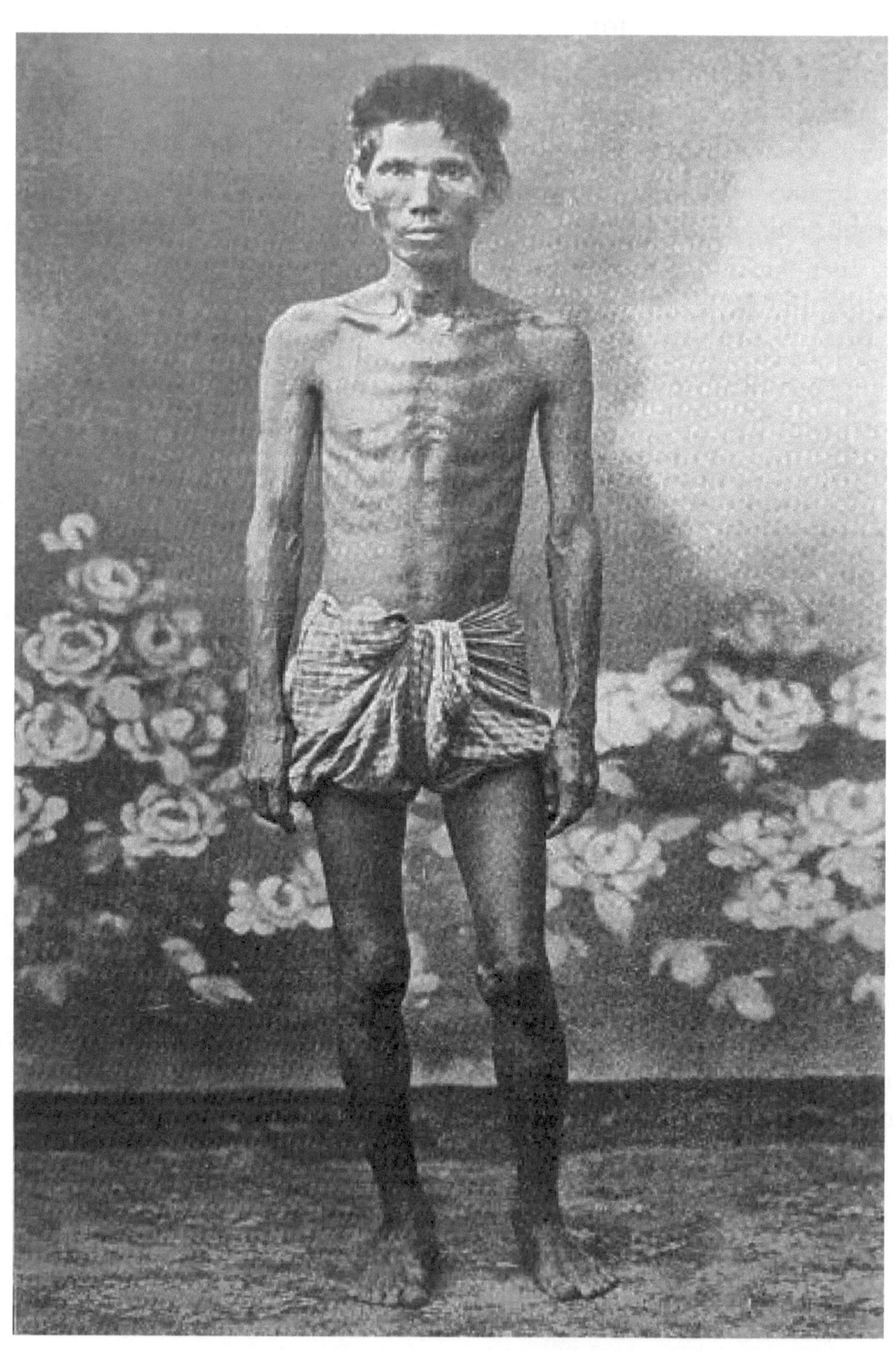

A Burman Cocaine Eater

Extreme poverty is frequently a cause of the habit. The abject wretch who becomes possessed of a few coppers, realizing that the amount will be insufficient for a square meal, buys an innocent looking packet of cocaine, and mixing it with a small quantity of the lime-paste used by betel-chewers in their quids, smears the mixture on his gums, and slowly swallows the saliva. Gone are the cravings for food; a feeling of pleasant warmth suffuses his wasted body; he feels equal to any exertion. Images are distorted to immense proportions; the stick he holds becomes a club of huge dimensions, and he takes great pride in his ability to wield it so easily; an empty jam-tin lying near assumes the proportions of a five-gallon milk-can; and he takes great pleasure in showing his agility in jumping high over the threshold of the door! In all, he considers himself to be a very fine, powerful, prepossessing fellow indeed—until the effects wear off, and he once more sets off to beg or steal the price of another dose of this elevating narcotic.

I once knew a European who was addicted to this drug—he injected it—and a more pitiable object it would be difficult to conceive. He was a dentist by profession, and the last I heard of him was that he had died by his own hand, a frequent termination of this habit, which produces in its last stages, a sort of morbid, gloomy, mania or insanity in its victims. This individual was the victim of all kinds of hallucinations, and under the influence of the drug, was a fluent, and often convincing, liar. He invested himself with numerous medical degrees; he went in terror of imaginary assailants; and he had a fixed idea that his meagre belongings were the envy of murderous burglars. So much so, that on more than one occasion he fired off the revolver he carried by day, and placed under his pillow by night, at imaginary intruders, to the no small risk of other occupants of the house he lived in. The tales of personal adventure he related, the accounts he gave of deadly combats with men twice his puny size, his stories of his property and wealth at home, were the wonder of all to whom he told them, and who were unable to discover in him the characteristic effects of the fell drug cocaine.

We are unfortunately without complete information about cocaine, but we know enough about it to realize that the habit is spreading with the rapidity and devastating effects of a conflagration over the world. As far as India and Burma are concerned, the law is stringent and severe, and the Dangerous Drugs Bill, which was lately occupying the attention of the Home Government, goes far on the road to bringing things at home into line with India and Burma.

The Germans discovered a method by which cocaine can be manufactured synthetically; and bogey hunters will discover a deep plot to undermine the physique and morals of Indians when they are told that the synthetic manufacture of cocaine is, to all intents and purposes, a state-aided industry. It is classed as an industry, and as such receives the spirit used in the preparation of the synthetic drug, duty-free. Ninety per cent. of the cocaine imported into this country before the war came from Germany.

It would probably surprise the Darmstadt firm, which purveyed almost all the cocaine that came to Burma, if they knew that their drachm-phials, neatly capsuled, and labelled "Cocaine Hydrochloride," ought really sometimes to have been labelled "Antefebrin," for that indeed is what a great number that were seized by the authorities contained. In appearance, cocaine and antefebrin are hard to distinguish from one another; and for a long time the results of analyses led the authorities to suppose that the manufacturers were defrauding their eastern constituents; but the discovery of a complete plant consisting of phials, labels, capsules, and a large quantity of antefebrin, eventually cleared the name of the doubtless reputable manufacturers, and fastened the guilt upon local swindling smugglers.

Chapter XII.

Hemp Drugs.

Like the poppy which is cultivated for opium, the hemp plant, *cannabis sativa*, is grown for *ganja*, *bhang*, and *churrus*, all highly intoxicating drugs; and for its bast fibre which makes such excellent rope.

The history of the plant is interesting, but no more than a very brief allusion to it is necessary here. The first mention of hemp occurs in Chinese literature, about the twenty-eighth century, B.C., when the hemp-seed is mentioned as one of the five or nine kinds of grain. It is mentioned merely as a "sacred grass" in the *Athavaveda* about 1400 B.C. But the narcotic properties of the plant, with which we are chiefly concerned, do not seem to have been known until the beginning of the fourteenth century A.D. In a Hindu play written about the sixteenth century A.D., Siva brings down the *bhang* plant from the Himalaya, and gives it to the worshippers of himself. Of more recent evidence, we have the statement of the Emperor Baber, who tells in his *Memoirs* (1519 A.D.) of the number of times he had taken *Maajun*. John Lindsay, in his *Journal of Captivity in Mysore* (1781), relates how his soldiers were made to eat *Majum*; and lastly, De Quincey, in his *Confessions of an English Opium-Eater*, speaks of *Madjoon*, which he inaccurately states is a Turkish name for opium.

The hemp plant belongs to the diœcious order of plants, of which the Hop is another member. That is to say, the flowers, male and female, are borne on separate shrubs. The male hemp plants die early, or are removed by hand, an operation which requires expert knowledge of the two plants; but the female is tended and looked after until the flowering tops are developed. These are then collected and dried, and are called *ganja*. The leaves, stalks and trash are collected, and this is called *bhang*; while the resin (which is collected by hand, like opium, or sometimes, made to adhere to the clothes, or special leather garments, or even the skins of men who walk up and down among the growing plants and is then scraped off and worked up into a mass by rolling and pressing) is called *churrus*. This is really the active principle of the hemp. Its presence in the flowering tops, leaves and stalks giving *ganja* and *bhang* their narcotic properties; and *churrus* is therefore more potent in its intoxicating effects than either *ganja* or *bhang*.

Ganja is a greenish-brown conglomeration of what looks like half-dried, tightly pressed grass; *bhang* is somewhat similar in appearance, but looser in form; and *churrus*, the resin itself, is a greenish-brown, moist mass. When it has been kept some time, it becomes hard, friable, and of a brownish-grey colour. When it assumes this condition and colour, it is inert. All have a characteristic, faintly pungent, odour, and but slight taste. It is interesting to note that the word *churrus* means a "bag" or "skin." It is believed that the name was applied to the drug from the skins or bags in which it used to be imported in olden times, from Central Asia.

Indulgence in hemp in India is as common as betel-chewing and tobacco smoking. It is, in one or other of its forms, either smoked, or eaten. (The sweetmeat *Majum*, is compounded from *bhang*, honey, sugar, and spices. Sometimes it is infused in cold water to which butter is added. The butter in time takes up the active principle of the drug, and is eaten.) And it is computed that the votaries of hemp, in one or other of its many forms, number three millions! There is great diversity of opinion as to whether hemp is gravely harmful to its consumers, or whether it is merely an undesirable form of indulgence without any evil permanent effects. The Indian Hemp Drugs Commission, which examined the whole question in detail, was of opinion that it was harmless if indulged in moderately, but that the gravest results must follow upon intemperance in its use. As regards its being a fruitful cause of insanity, the evidence of alienists was taken, and the statistics of all the large asylums for the insane in India were examined; but "only 7·3 per cent. of lunatics admitted to asylums were those in which hemp could reasonably be regarded as having been a factor of importance. Moreover, the form of insanity produced yields readily to treatment," and as hemp has not got the same hold that opium has upon individuals, its discontinuance is easily effected and immediate restoration of the mental faculties comes about.

The moderate use of *ganja* increases the appetite, and produces a condition of cheerfulness. In excess, hallucinations, and a sort of delirium is excited, and it is in this aggravated state that a man may "run amok." This is the outstanding evil of the drug: to temporarily madden a man. But, for the fatal consequences which often ensue from running amok, people are apt to put the whole blame on the drug. May it not, however, be that a man whose desire it is to become reckless purposely resorts to the drug to hearten himself? I think it is very likely. It is often discovered, after a man has run amok, that he has for some time been broody or sulky, and suffering under some real or imagined wrong. That he should get desperate, and take in excess what he well knows to be is an excitant infinitely more powerful than alcohol, in order to carry through what he has been longing for some time to do, is not altogether unreasonable.

To digress from the subject immediately under discussion; it is common in discussing crime and its connection with drink, to hear the view expressed that drink is the cause of crime *primâ facie*; whereas it often happens that a person intent on revenge cannot bring himself to do his neighbour a mischief in cold blood and requires a little "Dutch courage" to tune himself up to the pitch of not caring for consequences. Too often the crime committed is the result of impetuosity; impetuosity exacerbated by drink. We never hear of offences against property being attributed to drunkenness; and yet, from the moral standpoint, the deliberate commission of theft or robbery is evidential of greater obliquity than the passionate striking of one's enemy with whatever comes to hand at the moment.

Medical Jurisprudence is crowded with instances in which hemp has been employed in the commission of crimes. A single instance, which came within the writer's personal experience, will however suffice. The Civil Surgeon of ... had gone out on tour leaving behind his wife and family of three small boys. The bedroom occupied by Mrs. Blank adjoined that usually occupied by the doctor, which contained a large, heavy iron safe in which was Mrs. Blank's jewellery and a large sum of money. That night, Mrs. Blank and the children retired to bed at the usual hour; but upon waking in the morning, she felt unrefreshed and languid. The children complained of a like feeling. Going into her husband's room, Mrs. Blank was shocked to find that the safe had disappeared, one of its heavy massive handles lay wrenched off upon the floor, and a twisted gun barrel near by had too apparently been used ineffectually as a lever. An alarm was raised, and the police called in. Mrs. Blank averred that the safe was too large and heavy for fewer than six powerful men to carry down stairs. That she had been drugged there could be no doubt; she had slept and the children had slept through the night undisturbed, and it was impossible to conceive how they could otherwise have done so, with evidences of such noisy activities abundant in the next room. The safe was never found, and the culprits were never brought to book; but the discovery of a small patch of cultivated hemp, on some land belonging to a man servant who was in the Civil Surgeon's employ at the time of the burglary, made the case clear, and the servant's complicity morally, if not judicially, certain.

*   *   *   *   *

L'Envoi.

A Persian Allegory.

Three men, one under the effects of alcohol, one under the effects of opium, and the last under the effects of hemp, arrived one night at the closed gates of a city. "Let us break down the gates," said the alcohol drinker in a fury of rage, "I can do it with my sword!" "Nay," said the opium eater, "We can rest here outside in comfort till the morning, when the gates will be opened, and we may enter." "Why all this foolish talk?" whined the one under the effects of hemp. "Let us creep in through the key-hole. We can make ourselves small enough!"

Appendix.

An Historical Note on Opium in India and Burma.

It is doubtful whether there is a more valuable drug in the Materia Medica than opium. Fundamentally, it is the dried juice of the *Papaver Somniferum* or white poppy, and although all varieties of poppy are capable of producing opium, the best comes from the white, and it is this variety that is systematically cultivated for the world's supply of opium.

Opium has been the cause of at least one war, namely, the war between England and China, and a perusal of the accounts of piracy in the eastern seas during the sixteenth century affords numerous instances of pitched battles between traders and pirates whose one object seems to have been to get possession of valuable cargoes of opium.

The cultivation of the poppy, as a garden flower at any rate, was certainly practised as far back as eight hundred years before Christ. Homer, who lived between 800 B.C. and 700 B.C.[6] mentions it in his Iliad.[7] Cornelius Nepos also mentions the poppy in Italy; when Tarquin indicated to the envoy sent to him by his son Sextus Tarquinius, what he wanted done to the

---

[6] Mahaffy, "History of Classical Greek Literature," 1-81.

[7] "Down sank his head, as in a garden sinks
A ripened poppy charg'd with vernal rains;
So sank his head beneath his helmet's weight."

Iliad. (Lord Derby's translation, VIII.)

chief inhabitants of Etruria, by striking down all the tallest poppies in his garden.[8]

Hippocrates, who lived in the fifth century before Christ, and who is famous as the founder of Greek medical literature, is the first to mention poppy juice, and the virtues of the poppy were undoubtedly known to him; but the physical effects of opium were not definitely mentioned until the first century before Christ, when Vergil, who lived from 70 B.C. to 19 B.C., writes of the "Poppy pervaded with Lethean sleep,"[9] and the "Sleep-giving poppy."[10] It may be mentioned in passing, that in Greek mythology Lethe is a river that flows through the regions of the dead, the waters of which, if drunk by anyone, cause oblivion in regard to their past existence.

In the first century after Christ, opium was known as a medicine. Opium is mentioned by this name by Pliny[11] and by Dioscorides[12] both of whom lived in this century and its soporific effect was well known. The poppy was cultivated for opium on the eastern shores of the Mediterranean, and as the bulk of the trade between Europe and the Indies passed through these countries, it is certain that this drug, whose value was known, must have formed a part of the trade, though not, perhaps, to such a great extent as to attract attention.

Early in the seventh century after Christ, the religion of Islam was established in Arabia. By the commandments of this new religion the use of alcohol was absolutely forbidden, and it is supposed that those who had been used to alcohol began to use opium and hemp drugs as substitutes, the fact that these two drugs were not explicitly mentioned being sufficient sanction, apparently, for their use. It seems certain that with the spread of Islamism, the use of opium as a stimulant became more widely diffused. The Arabs were at that time, to all intents and purposes, masters of the

[8] "Huic, nuntio, quia, credo, dubiæ fidei videbatur, nihil voce responsum est, Rex, velut deliberabundus, in hortum ædium transit, sequente nuntio filii: ibi inambulans tacitus, sum apapaverum capita dicitur baculo decussisse." Livy i., 54.

[9] "Lethæo perfusa papavera somno." Georg.: i, 78.

[10] "Soporiferumque papaver." Aeneid: iv, 486.

[11] "Natural History."

[12] "Materia Medica."

eastern seas. They made long voyages, and carried on a trade with India and China, and from contemporary literature it has been definitely established that it was the Arabs that introduced the poppy, and a knowledge of its properties, into China. It is probable that opium was used as a stimulant in India also, at this time, but nothing is definitely known about this, and the history of the production and use of the drug before the sixteenth century is obscure. There are many indications, however, that the opium habit came into India in the eighth century, when the Arabs invaded and conquered Sind; and as the habit spread with the wanderings of the Arabs, there is much in the surmise. From this time, up to the end of the eleventh century, the Mahomedan invaders brought the greater part of India under their rule or influence, and in Portuguese Chronicles, written in the sixteenth century, the cultivation of the poppy, the opium habit, the production of opium, and its export are talked of as established things. Authorities on India conclude, from the inherent reluctance of the Indian to rapidly adopt new habits or crops, that the opium habit, and the cultivation of the poppy for opium, must have taken at least three hundred years or so to develop over such large areas.

The Portuguese discovered the Cape route to India in 1488, but it was not till ten years later that they first crossed the Indian Ocean and appeared on the west coast of India. They visited all important places on the coasts, and the great Islands of the Malay Archipelago, and established themselves in many places. They were not welcome, however, and were treated as intruders by Oriental traders. Many and fierce were the encounters between the Moors, and Arabs, and the intruders, who were, in the greater number, buccaneers and pirates rather than merchants. Numerous references to opium occur in the literature of those times. Vespucci mentions "opium, aloes, and many other drugs too numerous to detail" in a list of the cargo carried by Cabral's fleet from India to Lisbon in 1501. In 1511 Giovanni da Empoli mentions the capture of eight Gujarat ships laden with opium and other merchandize; and in a letter written in 1513 by Albuquerque to the King of Portugal, he says "I also send you a man of Aden who knows how to work afyam (opium) and the manner of collecting it. If Your Highness would believe me, I would order poppies of the Açores to be sown in all the fields of Portugal and command afyam to be made, which is the best merchandize that obtains in these places, and by which much money is made; owing to the thrashing which we gave Aden no afyam has come to India, and where it once was worth 12 pardoes a faracolla, there is none to be had at 80. Afyam is nothing else, Senhor, but the milk of the poppy; from Cayro (*sic*) whence it used to come, none comes now from Aden; therefore, Senhor, I would have you order them to be sown and cultivated, because a shipload would be used yearly in India, and the labourers would gain much also, and the people of India are lost without it, if they do not eat it; and set this fact in order, for I do not write to Your Highness an insignificant thing."

Duarte Barbosa[13] (1516) makes several references to opium:—

> Duy (Diu): "They load at this port of the return voyage cotton ... and opium, both that which comes from Aden, and that which is made in the kingdom of Cambay, which is not so fine as that of Aden."
>
> Peigu (Burma): "Many Moorish ships assemble at these ports of Peigu, and bring thither much cloth of Cambay and Palecate, coloured cottons and silks, which the Indians call patola, which are worth a great deal here; they also bring opium, copper ... and a few drugs from Cambay."
>
> Ava: "The merchants bring here for sale quicksilver, vermilion, coral, copper ... opium, scarlet cloth and many other things from the kingdom of Cambay." D'Orta described Cambay opium as yellowish, while the Aden variety was black and hard, and apparently the better liked kind.[14]

A Dutchman named Linschoten,[15] in an account of his travels and voyages, in 1596, gives an exaggerated account of the effects of opium.

[13] "The Coasts of East Africa and Malabar," by Duarte Barbosa. Translated from the Spanish and edited for the Haklvyt Society by the Hon'ble H. E. J. Stanley in 1866.

[14] Paper by Dr da Cunha in the transactions of the Medical and Physical Society of Bombay, 1882.

[15] "Discourse of voyages unto ye Easte and West Indies."

He says: "Amfion, so called by the Portingales, is by the Arabians, Mores (Moors) and Indians called affion, in Latin, opio or opium. It cometh out of Cairo in Egypt, and out of Aden upon the coast of Arabia, which is the point of the land entering into the Red Sea, sometimes belonging to the Portingales, but most part out of Cambaia, and from Deccan; that of Cairo is whitish and is called Mecerii; that of Aden and the places bordering upon the mouth of the Red Sea is blackish and hard; that which come from Cambaia and Deccan is softer and reddish. Amfion is made of sleepeballs, or poppie, and is the gumme which cometh forth of the same, to ye which end it is cut up and opened. The Indians use much to eat Amfion, specially the Malabares, and thither it is brought by those of Cambaia and other places in great abundance. He that useth to eate it must eate it daylie, otherwise he dieth and consumeth himself. When they begin to eate it, and are used unto it, they eate at the least twenty or thirty grains in weight everie day, sometimes more; but if for four or five days he chanceth to leave it, he dieth without fail. Likewise he that hath never eaten it, and will venture at the first to eate as much as those that daylie use it, it will surely kill him, for I certainly believe it is a kind of poyson. Such as use it goe alwaise as if they were half asleepe. They eate much of it because they would not feel any great labour or unquietness when they are at work, but they use it most for lecherie ... although such as eate much thereof, are in time altogether unable to company with a woman and whollie dried up, for it drieth and whollie cooleth man's nature that use it, as the Indians themselves do witness. Wherefore it is not much used by the nobilitie, but only for the cause aforesaid."

Cæsar Fredericke,[16] a Venetian merchant, who travelled extensively in the East, writes, about 1581, an account of his voyages and some of his ventures: "And for because that at my departure from Pegu opium was in great request, I went then to Cambay, to employ a good round summe of money in opium, and there I bought sixty parcels of opium which cost me 2,000 and 100 duckets, every ducket at 4 shillings 2 pence...." It is interesting to note that one Ralph Fitch,[17] who travelled in the East from 1583 to 1591, visited Burma, or Pegu as it was called by voyagers then, writes that opium

[16] "Haklvyt's voyages," Volume IX, Asia, Part II.
[17] "Haklvyt's voyages," Volume X, Asia, Part III.

from Cambay and Mecca was in great demand. These references, and a great many more could be given, go to show that by the sixteenth Century opium was not only well known, but formed an important item of maritime trade in the East.

By 1612, the English and Dutch East India Companies had been formed. The Dutch had established a trading post or factory at Surat, from which they were afterwards expelled by the English Company, and both Companies had factories on the Hughli in Bengal. They were not friends, and often fought, but they combined against the Portuguese and Spaniards who had appeared on the scene a hundred years before, and who looked upon all trade from India round the Cape as their monopoly. By the beginning of the seventeenth century the Portuguese had lost almost all their possessions in India to the Dutch, and their trade had weakened and diminished to a point which rendered them almost negligible as competitors in trade. At this time, several European nations granted monopolies of trade to the Indies, and the French and the Danes now came on the scene. It was found impossible, however, to keep out private individuals who sought to set up trading factories on their own account, despite monopolies, and swarms of these adventurers came in to trade in all the valuable articles of merchandize, including opium. They looked upon force as their only law, and their depredations on the seas perpetrated against the Indian sailors brought about the speedy decay of the old native sea-trade.

Although the English Company established a predominance over the Dutch in general trade, the latter maintained a lead in the trade in opium. They exported it to Ceylon, Malacca and the Straits, and it has been ascertained from contemporary chronicles that the Dutch had attempted to arrange with Indian Princes to monopolize the export trade of opium to China. In this, however, they failed, for the Portuguese, who had always had a monopoly of the export of Malwa opium, still held possession of their ports on the Cambay Gulf, and so were in a favourable situation for this trade.

In those days, as in these, Europeans did not come out to the East for the sake of their health. They came out with only one object, and that was to make money. Times have not changed since then. It was not unnatural therefore that they should look about for as speedy a means of amassing a fortune as possible, and found opium. Opium was to be got cheap in exchange for the merchandize with which trading ships came laden to the East. It was portable and durable, and as it was in great demand in the countries east of India it constituted an excellent substitute for money with which were purchased silks, tea, spices and pepper for which there was a great demand in Europe. It is probable that this demand for opium stimulated production and increased the output of opium in India, specially since the entry of the Europeans into the field of commerce in Eastern waters killed the native sea-trade which used to bring opium from Turkey. This increase in the output of opium must not be held to indicate an increase in consumption, as has been made out by some. On the contrary, it may be inferred that a decrease was brought about by the introduction of tobacco in the seventeenth century. When tobacco was unknown and the use of alcohol prohibited to Mahomedans, and looked upon as disgraceful by Hindoos, it is likely that the opium habit was more widely prevalent.

There was little change in the condition of affairs during the greater part of the eighteenth century, but a gradual increase in the demand from China about the middle of this century came about from the substitution of opium smoking for the smoking of tobacco.

The next stage in the history of the subject begins with the occupation of Bengal by the British East Indies Company in 1758, but it is first necessary to briefly outline how matters stood prior to it in connection with the production and sale of opium under Moghul administration.

No restrictions were imposed upon the cultivation of the poppy, and the agriculturist was as free to cultivate it as any other crop. He could sell his opium to whom he pleased, though generally he sold it to the money-lender who advanced him the money with which to begin cultivation ... a practice which obtains to this day in places to which the co-operative movement has not as yet spread. The opium produced was made over to the money-lender at a fixed price, but the rate at which the money-lender disposed of this opium was regulated only by the demand by European traders, and high prices were obtained. It is very natural that the native rulers of the day should have wished to participate to some extent in the huge profits made by these private traders, and a system was introduced by which a certain part of the profits on opium was paid into the State treasuries. This was willingly paid, as the burden was borne by the cultivator. As soon as the system came into force, the money-lenders formed a ring, and regulated the price paid by them for opium to cultivators, and took care to fix it at such a rate that the State demand did not deplete their own purses too much. As time went on, the confusion of the Moghul Empire, which began and ended, in the quarrels of Suraj-ud-Dowlah, did away to some extent with these rings, but custom and tradition are so strong in India, particularly when supported by men of substance, that when we occupied Bihar, a ring of wealthy opium dealers were found to be exercising an unauthorised monopoly in Patna opium which we were in too insecure a position to break.

This is how matters stood. But for some time before, the general confusion of the Moghul Empire, and its weakened authority, brought about a state of turmoil and disorder which obliged European merchants to raise troops, and convert their factories into garrisoned fortresses. Clive's victory over Suraj-ud-Dowlah at Plassey in 1757, however, brought things to a head, and established the British Company as military masters in Bengal. Suraj-ud-Dowlah was dethroned, and Mir Jaffer was set up in his place, the administration being confided to him under the general control of the Company. But this form of dual government resulted only in the oppression of the people, and general maladministration. The servants of the Company had always been allowed the privilege of private trade, and in this state of affairs they had unique opportunities for trading with the greatest advantage to themselves. Opium was, of course, exploited to the full, and when, what was known as the Patna Council, a number of the Company's servants, whose business it was to look after the Company's interests in Patna, discovered the existence of the opium ring, they were not long in appropriating its functions, and the very solid financial advantages it possessed. It is, perhaps, as well to explain that all this was done for the benefit of the several members of the Patna Council, and not on behalf of their employer. But the Council found that to avoid trouble it was necessary to admit the Dutch and French Company's servants who were naturally anxious to share in this unauthorized trade, and they very wisely admitted them, but to a minor share only.

In 1773, Warren Hastings was made the first Governor-General, and one of the first reforms he undertook was the suppression of private trade among the Company's servants, and of all irregular and unauthorised monopolies. When the Patna opium monopoly came to be examined, it was found to involve important considerations, and, after a full discussion in Council, it was decided not to set it free, but to make it a source of revenue to the State. It is to be expected that there were many against this, and various arguments were offered against the measure, but these were met satisfactorily; the Moghul monopolies had existed for years, and there was nothing novel in the creation of one properly regulated. Besides, the cultivators would be better treated, and would be less at the mercy of private traders and interlopers. The argument that if left free, more opium would be produced, was answered by Warren Hastings holding that increase was undesirable in the case of a pernicious luxury. Strangely enough, a strong line of opposition was taken by Francis, who was against all monopolies on general principles, and by the Board of Directors of the British East India Company, on the score of its being a form of oppression. They suggested leaving the trade free, subject to a Customs duty. His non-compliance with these instructions was one of the articles of Warren Hastings' impeachment later: "That this monopoly was a despotic interference with the liberty of the ryot, and that he should have complied with the Directors' suggestion."

The working of this new monopoly did not differ in essentials from the old form. The opium was collected from the cultivators by a contractor, but instead of its being handed over to the Patna Council, it was taken to Calcutta, where the bulk of it was sold by auction to the highest bidder. The balance was divided between the Dutch, French, and the commercial side of the British East Indies Companies at average auction prices.

The revised conditions under which this new State monopoly worked ensured the best opium coming into the Company's hands. It also did away with "middle-men," and all the profits which would have gone to cultivators if they had been allowed free trade. It is not unnatural, therefore, that some one should conceive the idea of securing the profits made by the sea-traders as well. In 1775, the revenue officers of Patna estimated that if the Dutch and French were kept out of the trade, 33,000 chests of Bengal and Bihar opium would be available for export, and suggested that the Company should export this to China, where it could be sold at an immense profit. The letter was considered in Council, but the suggestion was dropped by common consent without discussion. Warren Hastings, however, suggested an alternative of direct official agency, to the exclusion of the contractor, but this motion was lost by a majority, and the matter was closed. But in 1781 a state of affairs arose in which the Company found itself sadly short of money. We were at war with the French, Dutch, and Spaniards, at sea, and with Hyder Ali and the Maharattas on land. In consequence our ports were closed to foreign trade, the seas were not safe for ships flying the British flag, and all available merchant ships were employed in carrying grain and other supplies to Madras. Opium was unsaleable at Calcutta. It was under such conditions that it was decided to export opium to China, and, accordingly, the '*Nonsuch*' with 2,000 chests, was sent to the supercargoes at Canton, and the '*Betsey*' with 1,450 chests to the Straits of Malacca. A loan of 10 lakhs of rupees was raised on the cargo of the '*Betsey*,' to be repaid by bills of exchange on the Company from the Canton supercargoes. Another loan of 10 lakhs was raised from the public on the cargo of the '*Nonsuch*' on similar terms. The '*Betsey*,' after disposing of part of her cargo to advantage, was captured by the French and Dutch. The cargo of the '*Nonsuch*' was disposed of at a loss after much difficulty on account of the prohibition of the import of opium by the Chinese, and on account of the "immense quantities" of opium brought to Macao by Portuguese ships before the arrival of the '*Nonsuch*.' The loss on this venture was 69,973 dollars.

The Board of Directors, on hearing of this venture, which was undoubtedly an exception to the course of policy pursued by the East India Company in regard to the trade, while holding that there was no objection to the sale of opium in the Straits of Malacca, condemned the action of its representatives in exporting opium to China, where the import of opium was prohibited, as being beneath the dignity of the Company.

No more opium was exported to China, and the working of the monopoly remained unchanged until it was reformed, and the system of direct official agency was introduced by Lord Cornwallis. This system has remained in force up to the present.

Malwa Opium.—The first factory established by the British East Indies Company on the West Coast of India was at Surat in 1613. The Portuguese and Dutch had already established themselves here, and all of them participated in the opium trade to some extent. The Dutch were eventually expelled by the British who, as the Moghul power diminished, and the Maharattas became the rulers, assumed a commanding political position. But owing to their having a minor share in the territories along the coast, the major portion belonging to native princes and the Portuguese, although they could participate in the trade in Malwa opium, they were unable to assume a monopoly.

By the end of the eighteenth century, the State monopoly in Bengal had been firmly established, and good prices were being got for export opium. It was with a certain amount of apprehension therefore that they looked upon the trade in Malwa opium from the West Coast, and in 1803, this apprehension developing into something stronger, an order was issued prohibiting the export of Malwa opium from the Bombay ports. In 1805, the Bombay Government was asked to prohibit the cultivation of the poppy within the territories, some of which were newly acquired; but this order was demurred to, and the Directors concurred, holding that the cultivation was for opium for local consumption only, and not for export, and therefore unobjectionable.

At this time smuggling was rife. There were many routes, some very circuitous, by which the opium could be got to the sea-coast without trespassing upon the territories of the Company, but after 1818, when the third Maharatta war resulted in our getting possession of the whole of the Bombay sea-coast except Sind, how to get to the sea was a problem which confronted smugglers with increased complexity. But even so, the authorities were always faced with the danger of smuggled opium competing with Bengal opium and lowering its price. Treaties were therefore entered into with some of the States which had most reason to be grateful to us, by which they undertook to prohibit the export of the opium produced in their possessions, to check the cultivation of the poppy, and to sell what opium was produced to the agents of the Company at a certain fixed price. The arrangement did not differ materially from the system adopted in Bengal. But there were other States, such as Scindia and Jeypore, which refused to enter into alliances on these terms, and a time came when those who had signed treaties began to look upon the conditions they had agreed to as repressive. Merchants, who had been dispossessed of their profits by this system, were greatly in its disfavour, and there was no doubt about the disapproval of these measures by cultivators who were deprived of all the advantages of a competitive trade. In 1829 it was therefore decided to abandon this system in lieu of another, which required that a certain transit duty be paid on all opium passing through British territory to Bombay for export to China. This transit or pass duty was fixed at Rs. 175 a chest, but it varied, rising as it did in 1892 to Rs. 600 a chest. This system still exists in regard to Malwa opium.

All the details of legislation and regulation which concern this subject certainly come within the scope of this note, but their sketchy treatment is made necessary by considerations of space. A relation of the Chinese aspect would fill a volume, and no attempt is made here to describe it. But I feel that this note would not be complete without some reference to Burma.

That the use of opium was known in Burma long before British rule was introduced is evident from the records of Fitch and of Cæsar Fredricke, who visited Burma in the latter half of the sixteenth century. From the records of the Dutch East India Company also, Burma, it is seen, was looked upon as a good market for opium. It is very probable, therefore, that the luxury use of opium was practised by the Burmese people. The Buddhist religion prohibits the use of all intoxicants, and the edicts, issued by the State from time to time against their use, and later on, against opium in particular, appear to have been inspired by the Buddhist hierarchy. But it does not appear that the import of opium into Burma was prohibited by any measure of State prior to its annexation by the British. In the enquiry of 1891, Mr. Norton, Commissioner of Irrawaddy, wrote that, before the annexation of

Pegu in 1852, although capital punishment was prescribed for Burmans found with opium, yet opium was plentiful and easy to get at a cheaper rate than when he was writing. Several respectable Burmese gentlemen who were consulted during 1878 admitted that opium was freely used always.

Arakan and Tenasserim were annexed in 1826 after the first Burmese war and were attached to the Bengal Presidency for the purposes of administration under the Deputy Governor of Bengal, and it was not until 1862 that they, along with Pegu, were formed into the province of British Burma under the Chief Commissioner, Sir Arthur Phayre.

In 1826, the retail sale of opium in Bengal was conducted under the farming system. By this system certain tracts were farmed out to selected persons either by tender or by auction. These farmers were obliged to purchase Excise opium from the Government opium factories at a fixed price, which included the cost price and duty. This system was extended to Arakan and Tenasserim. As time went on, this system of opium farms was found to be bad and was replaced by the issue of free licenses to respectable persons. As Arakan was in a favourable position for smuggling, this system of free licenses was introduced there also, but Tenasserim, which did not afford the same facilities for smuggling, was allowed to retain the old system. That the system was unsatisfactory, chiefly on account of its tendency to cheapen opium, is apparent from a statement made by an old inhabitant of Akyab to Colonel Strover during the inquiry of 1891 that he had seen Government opium hawked about for sale in the streets during the early days of British rule. In 1864 Sir Arthur Phayre strongly condemned this new system, and in 1865 he drew up a set of rules which were brought into effect in 1866. The spirit of these rules is observed up to the present day in regard to the limit placed upon the quantity of opium which may be purchased by a licensee during a year for sale at his shop.

How things stood in Upper Burma at this time can be inferred from a report made to the Government of India by Sir Charles Crosthwaite under date 20th March, 1888. "On our taking over the country, stringent rules were enacted and somewhat rigorously enforced against the sale of opium. Many Chinese were flogged and otherwise punished for engaging in a traffic which, although it may have been nominally prohibited, was allowed to go on under the Burmese Government." From the statement of an official of the Burmese Government it would appear that the Burmese Government never openly recognized the opium traffic in Upper Burma; those persons only were punished who sold opium to Burmans. The Burmese Government admitted the existence of the traffic by levying customs dues on all opium imported into Upper Burma. In 1872, the British Political Agent reported that large quantities of Shan and Yünnan opium were being imported into Upper Burma and also smuggled. A Mr. Adams, of the American Baptist Mission, who was at Mandalay from 1874 to 1879, states that the *pôngyis* took great pains to suppress the consumption of opium by Burmans, with the hearty support of King Mindon, who was a great zealot in religion, much under the influence of the priesthood, and active in supporting every endeavour to enforce the law of prohibition. But this law was personal to the Burmans, and not a territorial law. Other races were under no restrictions in the matter of opium or liquor, and when our troops took Mandalay in 1885, enormous stores of opium were found secreted in the houses of Chinese merchants who said that they sold it regularly to Burmans. It is true that under King Thebaw's rule most of King Mindon's edicts became dead letters, and even *pôngyis* became addicted to opium.

The opium question attracted much interest, both locally and in England. The Anti-Opium Society took it up and much correspondence took place, which resulted in the total prohibition of opium to Burmans in Upper Burma and the rigid restriction of issues to them in Lower Burma. The reason for this is concisely put by Sir A. Mackenzie, Chief Commissioner of Burma, in a Minute: "I do not believe that opium in India or China does any great harm to the majority of those who use it, *i.e.*, to moderate smokers and eaters. But here, in Burma, we are brought face to face with the fact that the religion of the people specifically denounces the use of the drug; that their native kings treated its use as a heinous offence; that these ideas are so deeply rooted in the minds of the people that every consumer feels himself to be, and is, regarded by his neighbours as a sinner and a criminal; that the people are by temperament pleasure-loving and idle and easily led away by vicious indulgences; that they have little self-restraint and are always prone to rush into extremes. When a Burman takes to drink or opium he wants to get drunk or drugged as fast as he can, or as often as he can. All this seems to me to point to the necessity of special treatment."

9 789361 384998

Printed by Libri Plureos GmbH in Hamburg,
Germany